DISCARDED

JUN 2 6 2025

ELECTRONIC
SURVEILLANCE

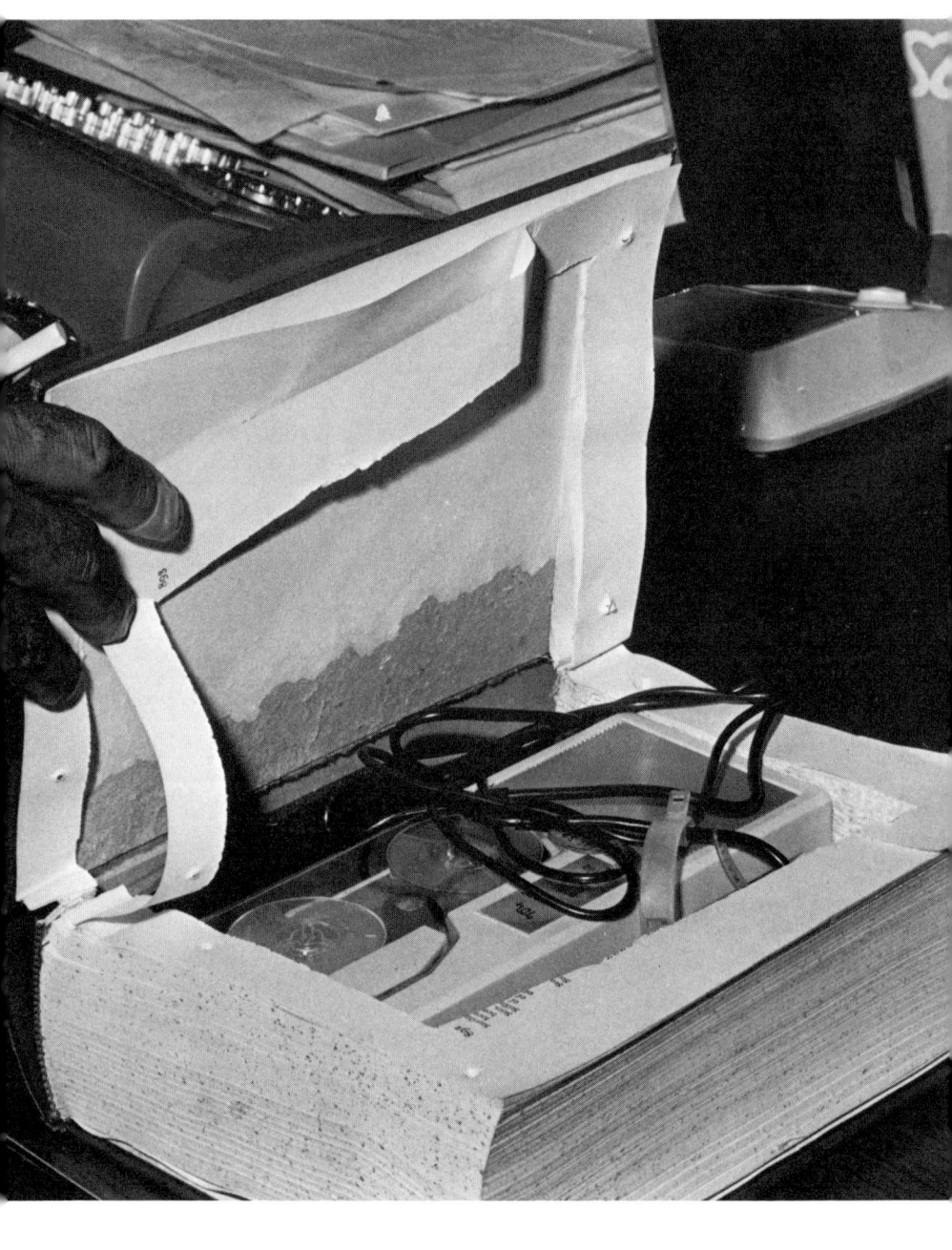

L. B. TAYLOR, JR.
ELECTRONIC SURVEILLANCE

FRANKLIN WATTS
NEW YORK | LONDON | TORONTO | SYDNEY | 1987
AN IMPACT BOOK

FRONTIS: NEARLY ANYTHING CAN SERV*
BUGGING DEVICE. THIS "BOOK" CONT*
BUILT-IN, VOICE-ACTIVATED TAPE REC(*

Photographs court*
UPI/Bettmann Newsphotos: pp. 2, 11, *
49, 51, 75, 77, 89 (top), 97, 102 (bc*
AP/Wide World: pp. 13, 21, 24, 40, 8*
Eye Dentify Inc.: p. 31; NASA: pp. *
CIA: p. 73; U.S. Air Force Photo: *
United Nations: p. 89 (b*

Library of Congress Cataloging-in-Publicatio*

Taylor, L. *
Electronic survei*

(An Impact*
Bibliogra*
Includes *
Summary: Examines modern electronic tools u*
surveillance involving federal agencies, private se*
defense, and espionage, including wiretapping *
listening devices, satellite cameras, and other*
spying d*
1. Electronic surveillance—Juvenile lite*
[1. Electronic surveillance] I.*
TK 7882.E2T39   1987   621.389   86-*
ISBN 0-531-1C*

Copyright © 1987 by L. B. Tayl*
All rights re*
Printed in the United States of Ar*
5 4 3

CONTENTS

Chapter One
The "Bug" Heard 'Round the World
9

Chapter Two
A Thousand Ears
15

Chapter Three
A Thousand Eyes
27

Chapter Four
Security Protection Systems
33

Chapter Five
Emerging Technologies
37

Chapter Six
To Catch a Thief
44

Chapter Seven
Prospecting from Space
53

Chapter Eight
Worldwide Weather Watch
63

Chapter Nine
The New Military High Ground
71

Chapter Ten
Toward a Police State
86

Chapter Eleven
Industrial Espionage
95

Chapter Twelve
Law of the Land
101

Chapter Thirteen
What Price Privacy?
110

Chapter Fourteen
Where Do We Go from Here?
119

Sources
124

Index
127

ELECTRONIC SURVEILLANCE

CHAPTER 1

THE "BUG" HEARD 'ROUND THE WORLD

Under the cloak of darkness in the predawn hours of June 17, 1972, five men broke into the Democratic National Committee headquarters on the sixth floor of a plush office building known as the Watergate in Washington, D.C.

Making his nightly rounds, an alert security guard named Frank Wills noticed that the door to this particular office had been tampered with. He immediately called the District of Columbia police. Three officers arrived shortly afterward, entered the headquarters complex, and found the five men crouching behind desks.

The five men were arrested and taken to the police station. There they were searched and were found to be carrying two cameras, forty rolls of unexposed film, a walkie-talkie, a telephone "bugging" device, tear gas pens, and over $1,200 in cash.

Four of the men were from the Miami, Florida, area, two of them Cuban exiles. The fifth man, James W. McCord, turned out to be an electronics surveillance expert who had worked for the U.S. Central Intelligence Agency (CIA) for more than twenty years.

Questioning of the men eventually led to the disclosure that they had illegally entered the office to place listening devices in it so as to pick up, from a distance, any conversations that took place within the Democratic headquarters. Actually, it turned out, they had placed equipment inside some days earlier, but one of the devices was not working properly, so they had gone back to fix or replace it.

What was the purpose of this strange mission? It was a presidential election year, and President Richard M. Nixon, a Republican, was running for reelection. In national politics, it helps to know what the strategy of the opposition party is, so plans can be made to counter it. By secretly bugging the Democratic party headquarters in 1972, Republicans hoped to learn every move the Democrats would make in the coming election.

However, what McCord and his four associates did constituted a criminal act. The resulting investigations into who authorized the entry and who else was involved in the scandalous act eventually led to the highest ranks of Nixon's administration. Ultimately, it led to the president himself.

Long after the Watergate break-in, it was learned that President Nixon had often taped conversations in the Oval Office of the White House, frequently without the knowledge of those who were being taped. For several months, a long legal battle waged over these tapes. In-

James McCord (below) testifies in front of the Select Senate Watergate Investigating Committee on his illegal surveillance activities at the National Democratic Committee headquarters in the Watergate complex.

vestigators contended that the tapes would settle the question of whether the president himself had been involved in trying to "cover up" his knowledge of the planned Watergate break-in.

Finally, the tapes were released, and they did, indeed, prove that President Nixon knew all along about the bugging of Democratic headquarters. Under threat of impeachment for this unlawful conduct, he resigned his office in August 1974, the first U.S. president in history to do so.

The Watergate bugging and the White House taping are but two dramatic examples of the technological era we live in today. Electronic surveillance, through such wide-ranging devices as listening "bugs" and unblinking camera "eyes" on earth and in space, has created a world in which even the most secret conversation or movement can be electronically recorded.

Evidence of this is all around us. Some of this evidence we can see and some we can't. Television monitors follow us throughout offices, department stores, and in banks and savings institutions. Police radar tracks us as we drive along roads and highways. Listening devices, some as tiny as the head of a match, can record what we say—on the telephone, in a building, or even in the middle of the field in the country or in a boat out at sea. And all the information obtained can be fed into computers and made available to analysts immediately.

Of course, many of these electronic eyes and ears are used for good purposes. For example, shoplifters in stores can be caught in the act by such surveillance techniques. Criminals or terrorists plotting dangerous acts can be found out. Bank robbers can be caught in the act, and spies can be trapped stealing or selling secret material.

Electronic satellites in space can warn of enemy troop movements, aircraft flights, or missile launches. They can also detect the detonations of nuclear weapons anywhere in the world as they occur.

President Richard Nixon displays on television transcripts of the tapes he made of confidential White House conversations.

But, unfortunately, electronic surveillance can also be used for unauthorized or unethical purposes. We can be watched and heard wherever we go without ever knowing it. And the users of electronic equipment can be anyone from government agents to private investigators. Our constitutional rights to individual privacy can be threatened.

As former U.S. Vice President Hubert H. Humphrey once said, "The right to privacy includes more than simply the right to be alone. Its most important characteristic is in exercising control over the number of participants in our communications—determining whether we wish our words locked away in a diary for no eyes but our own; restricted to conversation at dinner; or blazoned in the public media.

"We act differently if we believe we are being observed. If we can never be sure whether or not we are being watched and listened to, all our actions will be altered, and our very character will change."

Such are the dramatic ramifications of the age of electronic surveillance in which we live.

As you read on, you will be introduced to the various systems, devices, and technologies of electronic surveillance; how and why it is employed, both legally and illegally; the effects it has on us; and what, if anything, we can do about the situation.

CHAPTER 2
A THOUSAND EARS

A technological revolution has swept our world over the past quarter century. This has included incredible advances in electronics, semiconductors, computers, imaging, data bases, closed-circuit television, and electronic beepers and sensors.

The success of undetectable electronic surveillance has been greatly enhanced, too, by miniaturization of devices and systems. For example, transistors as small as the head of a wooden match now perform functions previously done by bulky radio tubes. They need only a fraction of the power and may be used with much smaller batteries. Complete receivers, transmitters, amplifiers, or oscillators can be built in a space no larger than a coin the size of a quarter. Closed-circuit television cameras can be made as small as a pack of cigarettes, and they can record scenes through an opening only a little larger than a pinhead.

Such ingenious devices can and are concealed virtually everywhere. They have been found in telephones, walls, furniture, clothes, jewelry, hearing aids, what have you. More than twenty years ago, a small transmitting device was found hidden in the olive of a martini. The "toothpick" protruding through the olive served as the antenna.

One of the oldest and most common means of electronic surveillance is the telephone "tap." Wiretapping, as it is frequently called, has been with us practically as long as we have had telephones and the telegraph. Basically, it refers to using a device to listen in on a telephone conversation. If you are talking to a friend on the telephone, for instance, and the line has been tapped, your conversation is possibly being heard and/or recorded by someone else.

Generally, there are two types of taps: the radio and the hardwire tap. In the case of the radio tap, the source may be a small radio transmitter using line power inside the telephone itself or in the mouthpiece. More typically, however, the radio tap is placed somewhere else along the line, such as in the terminal closet or junction box, where all the lines join to the external cables. Although these particular devices usually transmit only when the telephone is being used, more sophisticated equipment can be remotely triggered on and off whenever the telephone is expected to be used.

Hardwire taps may be connected nearly anywhere that radio taps are, including within the telephone. Contrary to what many people believe, both radio and hardwire are not always detectable, especially when they are installed by an expert. There are no clicks, buzzes, or other sounds in the background to give away a properly installed tap. In fact, there is no way to detect a tap on a line outside a controlled area without actual physical search, which is impractical. Even if the device is in the telephone itself, it often is difficult for anyone other than an expert to identify it.

For example, a complete, self-energized, solid state, miniature transmitter permanently fitted in plastic is about the size of an aspirin tablet, or smaller. By making only two connections, it can broadcast both sides of any phone conversation through FM radio. No batteries, induction coils, or other accessories are required, and it will not interfere with normal telephone operation.

Aside from routine tapping, another way to pick up telephone conversation is through the use of phone lines. There is a large family of electronic devices, called "infinity transmitters," or "harmonica bugs," which uses the lines and systems of switches and relays.

Passing audio themselves, they can be connected anywhere along the lines within the office, residence, or telephone itself, and are simply "called" by dialing the number from another phone and turned on by an audio tone signaling device. When the device is activated, the telephone never rings, but, electronically, it is as if someone answers the phone and, rather than hanging it back up, allows the party on the other end to listen in to conversations in the room where the phone is located. These devices disconnect automatically when the target telephone is picked up, so the target will never be alerted.

By altering the normal electrical characteristics of the telephone, it can be turned into a room listening device even when it is not in use. This is done by the connection of the telephone's mouthpiece or earpiece to the outside world via miniature radio transmitters or the phone's own wires.

Simple connections of components within the telephone, components that are readily available in TV and appliance stores, will permit room audio to pass as if the telephone receiver were left off the hook. And this can be done without affecting the normal operation of the phone.

A pen register is a small device that was developed to record the numbers dialed by a particular telephone. It is attached to the phone line exactly like a wiretap. But rather than recording conversations, it instead prints a tape listing the numbers called. This kind of information helps to determine what contacts have been made by those using the telephone while under surveillance.

A host of new technological developments in telephone service, paradoxically, is making it easier in some cases to tap into conversations. Consider the cellular

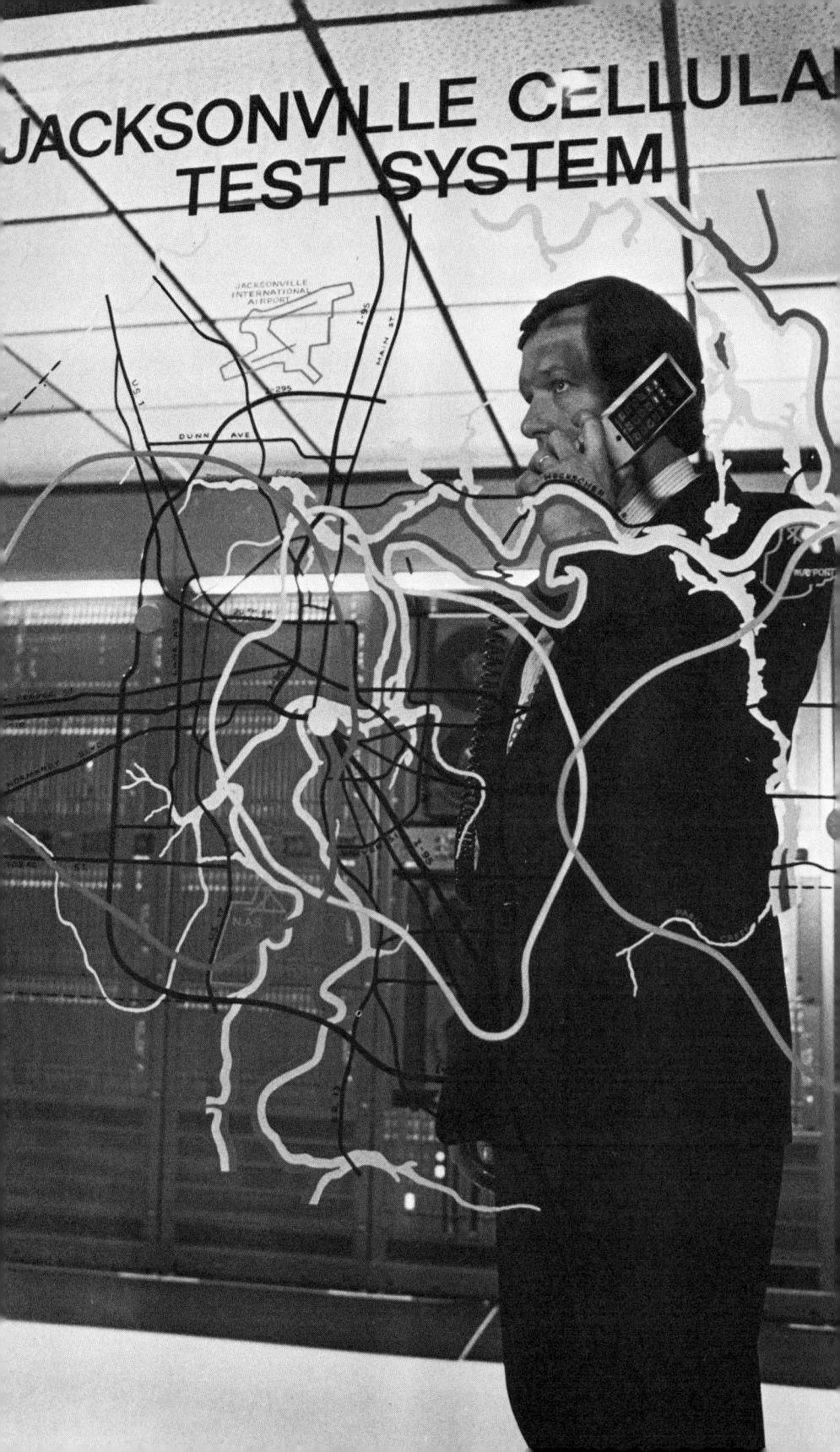

phone, which provides quality mobile service to users in vehicles across the country. As its costs go down, its popularity rises.

The problem is, these mobile units use radio to transmit messages between a phone and switching center. They are, therefore, relatively easy prey for eavesdroppers.

The cordless phone, too, has caught on in recent years as a hot consumer item. It enables a user to walk freely about his or her house, or even outside, while conversing. Cordless phones use radio to carry messages between the phone base station and the cordless phone handset. Oral messages thus are no longer transmitted from the receiver to the network via a line, but instead are transmitted between receiver and base station via radio. These transmissions can be picked up accidentally on a home or car radio and can also be easily intercepted by someone who wants to listen in. In fact, the Federal Communications Commission (FCC) now requires that such phones be labeled with a warning that conversations may be accidentally overheard.

A radiotelephone system has been under development for some time and may soon be available on the market. Cheaper than the cellular phone, this system will work either as a telephone or as a car-to-car radio. However, private conversations on the radiotelephone will be easy for third parties to tap, through such means as police scanners that are already available to the public.

Cellular phone systems are vulnerable to electronic surveillance techniques, as are cordless phones and other types of modern communication.

—19

As technology progresses, normal analog transmission is being converted to digital signals. The phone system of the future will carry digitized information (voice, data, and image) across wires, optical fibers, microwave radios, and satellite links. This will enable expanded service to customers. Experts point out that legal or illegal interception of digital signals is not significantly more difficult than for analog signals. They say the interceptor only needs a coder-decoder and knowledge of the modulation scheme.

More and more, computerized telecommunications switching equipment is collecting and storing information on telephone numbers dialed and the length of phone calls. While this is commonly kept for billing and administrative purposes, it also has monitoring capabilities. A detailed historical record of long-distance and sometimes local phone calls may now be kept by phone companies for three months. All this information can be made available to government officials with a court order. But, if a phone system is private, then the government can get access to the data without a subpoena, and the individual or individuals being probed may never be aware of it.

Although the telephone is the most common vehicle through which taps can be made, other modern telecommunications systems also represent serious invasion of privacy threats to users. Electronic pagers are one example. These have been used by doctors and traveling salespersons for more than twenty-five years. Their popularity has grown steadily in the 1980s, as lawmakers, lobbyists, repair personnel, business executives, and others began employing them to "stay in touch."

Today, it is estimated that more than two and a half million people in the United States use electronic pagers. The most popular unit is the "tone-in" pager, which beeps or vibrates to inform the user to call in for an important message. Tone voice pagers can broadcast a

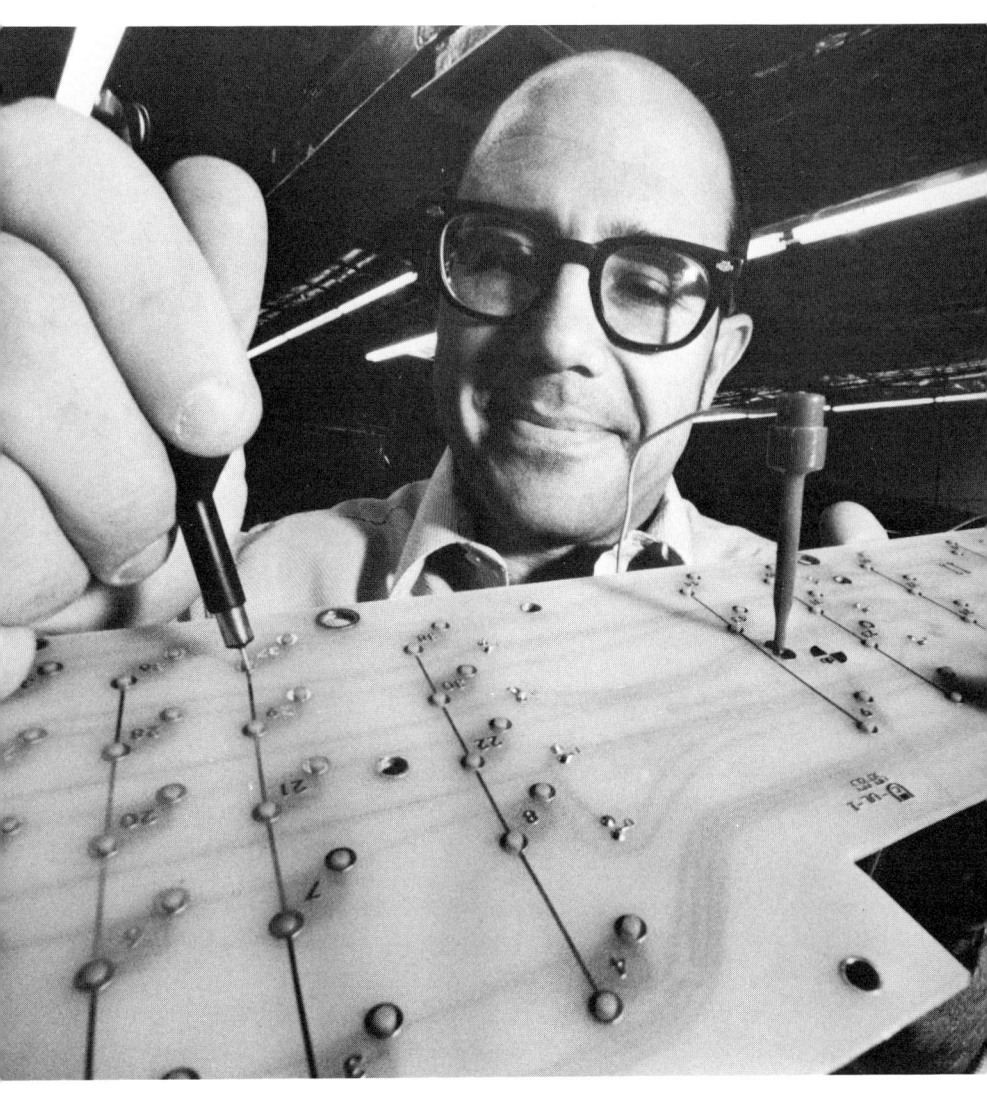

The circuit boards of today's "smart" telephones can hold more than 1,000 bits of information, including telephone numbers and personal data files. This information can all too easily be accessed by interested parties.

short voice message. The more recently introduced ten- or twelve-digit liquid crystal pagers can convey longer messages. And soon, a paging retrieval system will enable the caller's voice to be stored digitally for retrieval whenever the pager wearer is ready to receive it.

Most of these new paging systems can easily be monitored by anyone who has the proper portable telecommunications equipment. In fact, physical surveillance can be achieved much more readily and with far less risk than by such old methods as "tailing," or "shadowing," someone.

Interception of paging information, for instance, can reveal the recipient's location or activities. Anyone tuned to the same frequency of a paging system also can listen to any stored message. Further, paging radio technology has enabled the development of automatic vehicle location systems. By using the Long Range Navigation system (LORAN-C) of the Department of Transportation, it is possible to locate vehicles based on radio signals sent from the vehicle to a transmitter, then to a base station. With the use of an intelligent modem, information on the location of a vehicle can be communicated to a central point.

Another commonly used device in surveillance, often dramatized in spy movies and books, is the beeper, sometimes called the "bird dog." These are electronic transmitters that generate a series of pulses and are used as a tracking item, frequently by law enforcement agencies for covert operations.

About the size of a package of cigarettes or smaller, they can be concealed behind a vehicle's bumper, under the dashboard of a car, or virtually anywhere. They transmit a series of pulses every two seconds, which are picked up by a remote receiver. Beepers can track cars, trucks, ships, helicopters, or airplanes. They can tell whether a vehicle is parked or moving, what direction it is moving in, and how far away it is.

Still another popular means of secret surveillance is the family of electronic listening devices commonly referred to as "bugs." It was this type of tiny apparatus that the Watergate burglars were attempting to install in the Democratic National headquarters in Washington that eventually led to the resignation of President Nixon.

Bugs have been around for a long time. For example, in 1945, the Russians presented a wooden plaque of the Great Seal of the United States to ambassador Averell Harriman for display in the U.S. embassy in Moscow. Seven years later, it was discovered that a tiny listening device was implanted in the plaque. It was described as very small and with a microphone that, even today, is considered an extremely advanced piece of electronic equipment.

In the past twenty years, more than a hundred such bugs have been found hidden in U.S. embassies and in residences in Soviet bloc countries. They have been detected in telephones, radios, lighting fixtures, and furniture. They have also been concealed behind wallboards and imbedded in walls. The onrush of technology has spawned such fantastic advances in the miniaturization and sophistication of bugs that today it is nearly impossible to detect their presence without special electronic "sweeping" equipment.

Bugs can pick up conversations and transmit them over great distances through microminiaturized transistors as small as a lead pencil point. Tiny microphones can be hidden in a tie-pin, lapel pin, or a hearing aid, for example, to pick up and send face-to-face conversation. They can be concealed in a pocket, under a necktie, or even implanted under skin.

A microcircuit is an ingenious device made up of layers of metal 1/1000th of an inch thick sandwiched together. It draws power from radio waves in the air. Consequently, as long as a commercial radio station in the vicinity is on the air, the microcircuit will transmit.

This "buttonhole" microphone makes bugging easy. It can pick up all sounds within 10 feet (3 m), and the receiver can be up to 800 feet (240 m) away.

The transmitter is so small, it can be concealed in a slit in the side of a playing card, or placed inside wallpaper.

Eavesdropping can also be done through electrical wires, which can carry audio information from a room or building to an uninvited listener. Telephone, intercom, power, or even security alarm lines can be used.

Power lines, for example, are routinely run into even the most sensitive sanctuaries, such as business boardrooms or military code rooms. They provide excellent conduction paths for listening devices known as carrier current transmitters. Although such techniques have been employed for more than a quarter of a century, they are so obvious that they are often overlooked.

Through the use of these devices, very low-frequency signals are modulated using a microphone that receives room audio and passes it over the wires to a radio receiver. Highly reliable and difficult to detect, this method is most commonly used in office buildings and hotels and motels, where the receiver can be stationed in a nearby room or on a different floor. The devices themselves can be concealed in the wall, panelings, acoustical ceiling tiles, or other objects such as clocks or lamps.

A different category includes passive electronic devices that reflect radio energy of a specific frequency back to the source of that energy after being modulated with audio intelligence. These are high-frequency devices in the microwave region of the spectrum, or even later devices operating close to visible light. They are small, require no batteries or maintenance, and are the most difficult of all listening devices to detect.

More than twenty years ago, a Bell Laboratories engineer told a Senate investigating committee looking into espionage and surveillance techniques of a device that emitted a laser beam that would bounce back from a window pane and transmit the tiniest vibrations caused in the glass by sounds on the other side, or even light beams inside. Using this capability, a television screen could project a detailed picture, by day or night, of what was going on in a closed room without the occupants being aware of it in any way.

The committee also heard testimony that the Central Intelligence Agency (CIA) had devices that could turn an intercom, a regular phone, or even a simple electric-light circuit into a broadcast channel that would transmit private conversations anywhere in the world. It said the CIA could pick up at a distance of almost a hundred yards the vibrations of a window pane and overhear conversations inside, even if the room were totally soundproofed and without using any electrical or electronic devices.

Technology more recently has created an even more imperceptible eavesdropper—the infrared beam. When this invisible beam is focused from outside a room on any vibrating object inside the room, the conversation in the room can be "read" from these vibrations.

The largest group of electronic listening devices includes a wide-ranging family of miniature radio transmitters. These can be made to transmit on any frequency range and can be quickly "planted" in telephone mouthpieces, paintings or pictures, pencil holders, potted plants, or just about any object found in the ordinary office environment. The range of these devices—dependent upon their frequency and power—are usually from a few yards for the higher frequencies to a mile or more for the lower frequencies.

In short, super-sensitive sensors of a variety of sizes and shapes can pick up whispers in the midst of a forest, in enclosed rooms, even in a rowboat in the middle of a large, isolated lake. Your every word can be secretly heard and recorded—without your ever knowing it.

CHAPTER 3
A THOUSAND EYES

Another booming area of electronic surveillance involves the use of visual devices and systems—mostly cameras and closed-circuit television—which are used either by themselves or in conjunction with audio surveillance systems.

Again, technology has fostered this boom. The miniaturization of cameras has made them attractive tools for users who want to watch and record the movements of people without their knowing it.

The advance of fiber optics now permits the concealment of small cameras with the lens located at the surveillance site and the camera located at a distance. This is possible because of a "light pipe," a bundle of thin, transparent fibers that conducts light and visual images from a lens to a camera. With such devices, the watcher needs to enter a location only once. Film changing and retrieval can be done safely at a distance. With telescopic lenses, cameras can produce identifiable photos of persons or objects a great distance away, with high-quality results.

Newly developed miniature cameras can be concealed in anything from a briefcase to a lamp to a plant. Or they can be used through mirror windows—all completely without detection. It is thus easy for a person who has even brief access to an area under surveillance to install a tiny camera, leave, and return later to pick up the film.

Low-light-level television technology makes it possible to see in the dark. Infrared television cameras can also do this by detecting infrared radiation with a camera that is sensitive to such radiation, or by detecting infrared radiation and converting it to digital images. The system can then produce a detailed black and white picture.

One of the most recent advances is the development of machine vision systems. These combine video and computer technologies to allow computerized analysis of what is being captured by the camera.

Examples of electronic visual surveillance in use can be found everywhere in daily life. Banks and financial institutions run cameras continuously during operating hours to monitor both the teller counters inside and the automatic teller machines outside. Department stores, supermarkets, and all-night convenience stores regularly use such surveillance techniques to deter and detect shoplifting, and to compile a visual record of activity.

Airports all over the world routinely use cameras and television to ensure the safety of passengers and equipment. Many cities use closed-circuit television to survey street corners in high crime areas, on subway platforms, and at entrances to public buildings. The federal government employs electronic visual surveillance in many of its buildings to check people coming and going, and many businesses, plants, and factories do the same to monitor work activities.

And, all of these devices and systems are readily available on the market at reasonable prices. The following, from current security publications and catalogs, is a sampling of the literature descriptions of some of these items.

For $399.95 you can get "an affordable home or business security camera," which is advertised as being ideal for every location where there is money or valuables and the possibility of theft, vandalism, robbery, or personal harm. Among its touted features are self-developing film and easy-loading color film cartridge; high-speed film to freeze motion, crisp and clear; auto-focused wide-angle coverage and sequential photography; and a no-flash feature for holdups and suspicious persons (the camera automatically adjusts to any light, even total darkness).

Panasonic promotes a small business CCTV (closed-circuit television) camera that "provides high resolution video surveillance for virtually any size commercial establishment." It uses a single, half-inch vidicon tube for sharp resolution under low light conditions and is suggested for application in jewelry stores, gas stations, loading docks, and parking lots.

One company advertises a solid state camera "only slightly larger than a kingsize pack of cigarettes." It is said to have low power requirements and a lifespan of ten years or more. Openly, the company declares, "the rugged cameras are good for both covert and conventional video surveillance."

At the Tropicana Hotel in Atlantic City, New Jersey, two hundred cameras constantly scan the play in the gambling casino. Using super-sensitive RCA/Ultricon II tubes, they not only zero in on the players but can even "read" the cards in peoples' hands at blackjack tables. Such surveillance is used mostly to detect cheating. All gambling establishments have such advanced surveillance systems, mostly hidden from view.

Sony has developed a precision miniature video camera with a thumb-sized lens that fits snugly in the palm of the hand, yet produces high-quality pictures. Says its ad: "The photosensor elements are precisely arranged to present accurate geometric imagery that's equal to the demands of computer image processing." Such tiny cameras can be placed almost anywhere, even in the open, without being detected.

D/B Cameras of Fullerton, California, tells security equipment shoppers its cameras provide "the kind of proven surveillance you need . . . the sharp, clear film evidence you must have for strengthened security and a powerful deterrent." One model is advertised to "meet all the requirements of The Bank Protection Act," and a new Micro-Check System "provides a photographic record of a person and document with time and date on a single 16 millimeter film frame."

PSA Security Systems of Westminster, Connecticut, says it has one system that uses sixty cameras in ten buildings "which are integrated with alarms and gate openers, all remote controlled by a microprocessor which can be pre-set to train cameras to video tape any given area."

One of the most interesting electronic visual surveillance systems available today is marketed by a company called EyeDentify, Inc., of Portland, Oregon. It is used for what is called "access control," that is, to check the identity of someone entering a secured or classified area, such as a secret code room or a secret weapons area.

This system uses a low-intensity infrared light beam—light equivalent to that emitted from an opened refrigerator door—to perform a circular scan and 320 readings of the vessel pattern within the human eye.

The company says this is "more unique" as an identifying characteristic than a fingerprint. Every person, even an identical twin, has a totally distinct, stable eye vessel pattern. Unlike fingerprints and voiceprints, the internal structure of the eye can't be counterfeited or altered. Thus the system has an identity reliability that is said to exceed all other systems.

The process is simple. As the company describes it: "Each user focuses on a small pattern within the binocu-

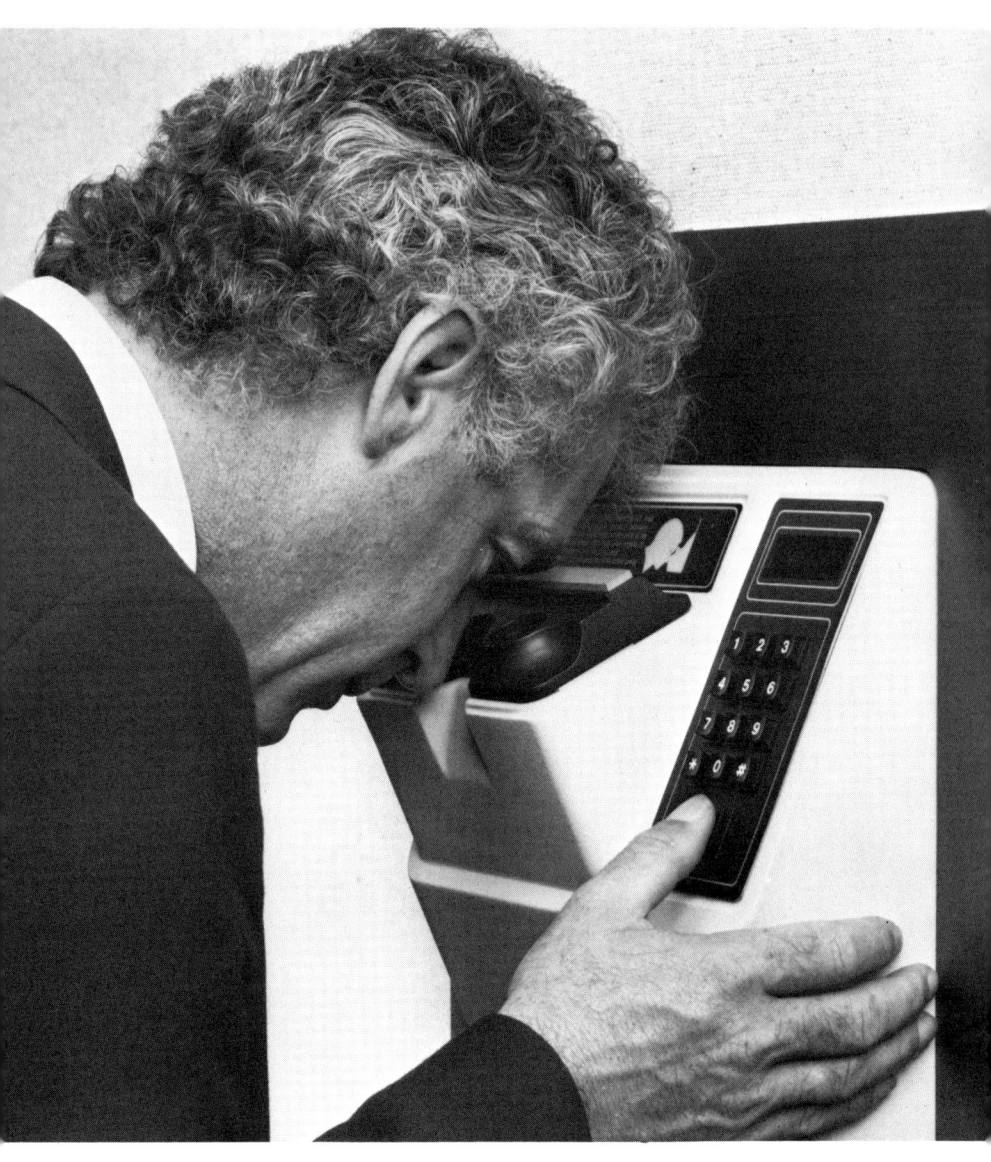

Identifying people by the blood vessel patterns in their eyes is one of the latest ideas in electronic visual surveillance.

lar unit and pushes a button. The system's microprocessor then compares the completed retinal scan with the eye signature already on file, in either on-board (computer) memory or remote data base. Once recognized, the persons are granted access to secured areas; others, however, are effectively kept out." The system can store up to 1,200 eye signatures at one site and can process an identification in one-and-one-half seconds.

Again, as with audio devices, there is no hiding from the prying eyes of visual electronic surveillance systems. They can see through everything, from brick walls to thick cloud cover, secretly following your every movement.

CHAPTER 4

SECURITY PROTECTION SYSTEMS

In addition to audio and visual techniques, a great array of protective alarm systems is being used by the U.S. government, state and local governments, and businesses large and small, to serve a variety of security purposes. Most of these involve some form of electronic surveillance.

Generally, there are two basic types of alarm systems. One is centrally located, and electrical protection circuits and devices send automatic signals to this point, where they are received and analyzed by security officers or operators. The central station serves as a clearing house, monitoring the signal end of the alarm system, providing a response, if necessary, to the signal, and supervising the functioning of the system.

The other type is called a local alarm system. Protective circuits and devices are connected to a visual and/or audible signal element located in the immediate vicinity of the protected area. If the area is penetrated, signals are dispatched and responded to by security personnel.

Such systems are generally used to protect large areas from spying, theft, or sabotage, usually because they can be operated more efficiently and inexpensively than a security patrol force. They are especially effective in areas where admission must be carefully controlled; facilities that, because of their nearness to other structures, activities, or property lines—require the use of alarms instead of physical barriers; facilities that are difficult or impossible to guard effectively because of terrain, physical hazards, or dangerous atmospheric conditions, and where other types of protection are not effective or practical; and facilities that are small or remote and do not require a full-time security officer yet need more than "lock and key" protection.

The military commonly uses electronic surveillance to guard against intruders at weapons storage facilities, at personnel bases, and at airfields, shipyards, and motor pools, among other areas. Utility companies use this electronic means of protection at power plants, electrical substations, and nuclear facilities. Businesses and industries use them to guard inventories and supplies as well as physical facilities. Prisons and correctional institutions can spot escapees instantly by electronic surveillance.

Here are some of the various types of systems and devices that are used for intrusion detection:

- photoelectric systems, which are triggered when a virtually invisible beam of light is interrupted;
- electromagnetic or microwave systems that pick up any "entrance" into their field;
- microphonic devices, which detect sound and vibration;
- thermal detectors, which are set off when a predetermined temperature limit is reached or the rate starts rising (the heat of the human body, for instance, could set off this alarm);
- electronic circuits, which transmit signals from the protected area to the signal apparatus;

- alarm or signal devices, which announce by audible or visual means any activity the system is designed to detect;
- closed-circuit television systems, with or without sound, which provide an electronically visual means of observing activity from a remote location.

A review of current security equipment literature reveals how advanced and sophisticated some of the systems are. Outdoor microwave sensors can detect any intrusion under any climatic condition—rain, fog, snow, dust, or temperature extremes. It does this by setting up an invisible field of microwave energy in a specified area. An alarm is set off if a person walks, runs, or crawls in that field. Yet the system is so sensitive that it will not be set off by small animals.

A new device in ultrasonic motion uses microprocessor-based signal processing and two principles of frequency shift detection to provide security. It memorizes characteristics of the protected environment so that any attempt at theft is immediately detected.

Ultrasonic perimeter-intrusion detectors are electronic devices that monitor and react to sound waves lower than the normal ear can hear. When installed, they are connected to a control instrument, and initiate an alarm signal when an intrusion is sensed.

Passive infrared sensors cover protected areas—especially rooms containing valuable items in offices and museums—by emitting electronic beams in pattern form. Any disruption of the beams sets off an alarm. The same type of security service is provided by photoelectric beam devices. Many of these systems can easily be disguised even in open view. Often, they appear on the wall as a thermostatic control unit. There is also a new device that will immediately detect any glass breakage, such as the shattering of a museum case housing a valuable object.

All of these systems and devices are difficult to detect, even by the most expert intruder. They have revolutionized the security industry and made protection of property a far more efficient operation.

CHAPTER 5

EMERGING TECHNOLOGIES

The rapidly emerging technologies, especially in the electronics and computer industries, have created vast fresh horizons for new electronic surveillance systems. This is particularly true in such areas as electronic mail and data base surveillance.

Traditionally, we expect, and with few exceptions receive, protection in our mail service. There have been occasions, generally illegal, where first class letters have been intercepted and read by government agencies and others. But for the most part, laws have guarded our privacy in written correspondence.

However, even here technology is changing things and opening new doors for those who wish to pry. One of the newest means of communication, for instance, is electronic mail. Through the computer, it now is possible to transmit and receive mail in electronic form.

This can be done by sending messages between computer terminals via telephone lines. In addition to terminal-to-terminal systems, this can also include such means as telegraph, telex, teletext, facsimile, voice mail, and mixed systems, the electronic signals of which may be transmitted by the postal service or couriers.

Here is a brief rundown of these techniques:

Telegraph—transmits one-way electronic messages along circuits within a network of central and branch telegraph offices. The messages are translated by the receiving operator into typed accounts that are hand delivered or telephoned to the addressee.

Telex—a teletypewriter terminal that translates messages into code. Each subscriber has his or her own telex line and number that a caller dials to send messages keyed into the terminal. The message then is sent to the receiver's automatic teleprinter. This is commonly used for international communications via satellite channels or trans-oceanic submarine cables.

Teletext—sends text and graphic messages sequentially in one direction over a television broadcast signal or cable, which are then received by a display terminal and exhibited on a display screen.

Facsimile—this system converts a page of text or images into data, which is scanned and translated into code. Regular telephone lines carry the message to a recipient's terminal for decoding and printing onto paper.

Voice mail—a computer-based system that digitizes voice from an analog signal to relay short messages. Like a digital phone-answering machine, messages can be stored and forwarded, edited, retrieved, or distributed to a list of users.

Electronic mail—an electronic message is transmitted between two or more terminals and remains in an electronic format. After transmission, the message can then be converted to a printed format for delivery by mail or courier service.

To use an electronic mail system, a personal identity number, password, the recipient's account number, and message are keyed into a terminal. This information is transmitted to a central computer for viewing by the recipient. These systems can send, receive, file, recall, edit, and store both text and graphic messages.

The main attraction of such systems is speed. With them, long messages, such as documents or working papers that normally would be sent by routine mail, can be dispatched much more quickly electronically. The U.S. Postal Service and commercial companies offer these systems, and many businesses and government agencies use them.

The problem is that such electronic messages can be intercepted with relative ease and their contents revealed to unintended receivers. This can be done at the terminal or in the electronic files of the sender; while being transmitted; in the electronic mailbox of the receiver; when printed onto paper copies before mailing; and when retained in the files of the electronic mail company. And, like so many other forms of electronic surveillance, the existing laws do not adequately provide protection for users.

Although few people ever consider it, they leave many telltale clues as to their movements and activities as they go about their daily business. By buying gas at the service station and clothes at a department store with credit cards; by making telephone calls; by bank card transactions; and by collecting unemployment insurance or food stamps, we leave records behind that can be traced, collected, and analyzed.

All this is done with computers. Every time anyone interacts with a retail, financial, educational, professional, governmental, or other agency, an electronic record is kept. Before computers, when records were kept on paper, it was too costly and too slow to try to put together

Using a hand-held computer, a person can now send telex messages to anywhere in the world by telephone—and also have these messages read by unwelcome eyes.

an activity "profile" of someone by matching records. With the computer, however, this can be, and is, done routinely. Electronic "linkages" are used to conduct surveillance of individuals by investigative, law enforcement, and other government agencies, as well as such private institutions as credit firms.

The U.S. Office of Technology Assessment reports that one example of a federal institution with a computerized record system that could be used for surveillance purposes is the FBI's National Crime Information Center (NCIC). Among other things, the center maintains an "electronic bulletin board" of wanted persons, missing persons, and persons with criminal records. This can be accessed by law enforcement and criminal justice agencies across the country, to find out whether particular individuals are listed as wanted or missing or have a prior criminal record. In some instances NCIC has been used to track individuals who had not formally been charged with a crime and did not have an outstanding warrant against them for a federal offense.

Another example is the U.S. Government's Treasury Enforcement Communications System (TECS), which includes a wide range of information on persons suspected of or wanted for violations of U.S. customs or related laws. This system maintains computerized records on more than two million people. But even these numbers pale when compared to the U.S. Immigration and Naturalization Service, whose Central Index System has files on 21 million aliens and naturalized citizens in the United States and whose Non-Immigrant Information System keeps tabs on 24 million temporary visitors to this country.

Overall, the Office of Technology Assessment identified eighty-five computerized record systems operated by federal agencies for law enforcement, investigative, and/or intelligence purposes. Together, these systems include about 288 million records on approximately 114 million persons.

Extremely rapid screening of mug shots and fingerprints is possible thanks to large databases of information, microfilm, and computers. What once took days now takes only minutes or even seconds.

The departments of Justice and Defense have by far the largest number of systems and records. Justice reports 15 systems, with about 241 million records on 87 million people. Defense has 18 systems, with about 29 million records of 22 million people.

And none of this includes the countless millions of records kept by stores, businesses, private industry, and credit agencies. These records may contain personal and sensitive information about individuals, all of which, theoretically at least, are available through data base surveillance techniques to anyone with computer access to the information storage systems.

CHAPTER 6
TO CATCH A THIEF

Who uses all of these electronic surveillance systems and devices, and why do they use them? Without question the two largest users are industry and the U.S. government, followed by state, county, and municipal governments, and small businesses. But the miracles of modern technology have made a large part of this electronic arsenal affordable to the general public, and today stores selling such paraphernalia are springing up all over the country.

But let's begin with the U.S. government. Uncle Sam is the greatest single collector of information about the individual. The Census Bureau alone collects and analyzes mountains of data about people. The Internal Revenue Service maintains a vast reservoir of facts and figures about the average person's private affairs. And some of this information, including the information on tax returns, is subject to inspection by all departments and agencies of the federal government and by members of Congress. Most people are not aware of this fact.

Literally tons of information are amassed by the Department of Health and Human Resources, which must keep tabs on millions of people for such massive programs as Social Security, Medicare, and the food stamps program. The same is true for the Department of Housing and Urban Development, the Defense Department, the Justice Department, the Labor Department, and just about every agency of the federal government. Most of these bodies employ electronic surveillance techniques to gather some of their data.

In a recent report published by the Congressional Office of Technology Assessment, the top fifteen federal agency users are as follows: The Drug Enforcement Administration, Department of Justice; the Federal Bureau of Investigation (FBI), Department of Justice; the U.S. Customs Service, Treasury Department; the U.S. Air Force, Department of Defense; the National Park Service, Department of the Interior; the Internal Revenue Service, Treasury Department; the Criminal Division of the Department of Justice; the U.S. Forest Service, Department of Agriculture; Inspector General, Department of Agriculture; Agricultural Stabilizations and Conservation Service, Department of Agriculture; the U.S. Army, Department of Defense; the Fish and Wildlife Service, Department of the Interior; the U.S. Marshals Service, Department of Justice; the U.S. Mint, Treasury Department; and the Bureau of Alcohol, Tobacco, and Firearms, Treasury Department.

Conspicuously absent from this list is the Central Intelligence Agency (CIA), which is alleged to be one of the most prolific users of electronic surveillance. However, most of its operations, like those of the National Security Agency and the Defense Intelligence Agency, are secret.

In times of national emergencies, such as war, government use of surveillance increases greatly. In congressional testimony, for example, the FBI revealed that it had performed more than 7,000 national security surveillance operations between 1940 and 1960, the period covering the Second World War, the Cold War that followed, and the Korean War.

The Treasury Department installed over 10,000 wiretaps between the years 1934 and 1948. In our current era of world unrest, nuclear weapons, and international terrorism, it is only reasonable to assume that usage by the CIA and other intelligence agencies is extensive.

What types of systems and devices are used? Of thirty-five federal agencies responding to the Office of Technology Assessment study, here is a rundown of the most popular means either in current or planned use. The number of agencies using, or planning the use of, each type of electronic surveillance follows in parentheses: closed-circuit television (29); night vision systems (22); miniature transmitters (21); radio receivers (scanners) (20); vehicle location systems, such as electronic beepers (15); sensors, including electromagnetic, electronic, and acoustic (15); telephone taps and recorders (14); pen registers (14); telephone usage monitoring (10); computer usage monitoring (6); electronic mail monitoring or interception (6); cellular radio interception (5); pattern recognition systems (4); satellite interception (4); expert systems/artificial intelligence (3); voice recognition (3); satellite-based visual surveillance systems (2); microwave interception (2); and fiber optic interception (1).

The basic reason the U.S government uses electronic surveillance technology, as stated in the report, is "for monitoring the movement, activity, conversation, or information pertaining to individuals or agencies in which the agency has an investigative, law enforcement, and/or intelligence interest."

The major targets of government surveillance are drug dealers and illegal gamblers. That is, they are the major targets of *known* surveillance. Because the covert actions of the CIA and other national intelligence agencies are cloaked in secrecy, no one knows just how much attention is focused on suspected spies and terrorists.

According to experts, electronic surveillance—particularly wiretapping and bugging—is used because it has proved to be effective in the following instances:

- in recording transactions involving narcotics or other contraband, usually transactions between undercover agents or informers and suspects. A famous example of this in the early 1980s was the use of closed-circuit television cameras by the FBI to record an alleged drug deal between federal agents and famous car manufacturer John DeLorean (later found innocent by a jury).

- in recording bribe offers to government agents or public officials. This was exemplified in the FBI's "sting" operation where federal agents, posing as foreign officials, offered large amounts of money to members of the U.S. Congress in exchange for legislative "favors." This, too, was recorded by hidden TV cameras

- in recording bets placed by undercover agents or informers, or their conversations in suspected gambling areas

- in coordinating raids and arrests, and in providing protection for undercover agents and informers

- in maintaining surveillance of the homes or offices of suspected criminals.

How effective are such techniques? Again, this is difficult to assess because so much of the surveillance, especially in national security cases, is not revealed to the public. The report of the Office of Technology Assessment, however, cites that in 1984, "an average of about 25 percent of intercepted communications was reported to be incriminating in nature, with 2,393 persons arrested as a result and about 27 percent of those convicted."

Security is big business with private industry, too. Companies large and small spend billions of dollars a year on security measures, including everything from armed guards to bank vaults to attack dogs. A rising percentage of this enormous amount of money is spent for electronic surveillance systems. The major purchases include:

- Closed-circuit television. Sales were $110 million in 1983 and are expected to reach $620 million by 1995.

- intrusion detection systems. These totaled $435 million in 1983 and are projected at $1.4 billion by 1995.

- electronic article surveillance systems, such as cameras and beams designed to control theft losses in stores. These are estimated to reach $650 million in sales by 1995.

These projections were published by Security World Magazine.

Businesses have found that in more and more instances, such systems are not only more efficient but also cost effective. And, electronic systems can often do the job where it is impractical or too expensive to employ humans.

For example, department stores, convenience stores, shops, boutiques, and other retail establishments use closed-circuit television and other cameras to keep a constant watch on their inventories. Although most store managers will tell you that the basic purpose of this visual surveillance is to discourage shoplifting, the fact is they are actually used more to stop employee theft, which is a bigger problem.

Security studies say that employees steal two to five times as much as shoplifters, resulting in losses of $4 billion a year to retailers. One survey of 9,000 employees found a third of them admitting they stole from their companies. In many reported instances, just the pres-

This split photo shows both the video camera and the closed-circuit TV monitor used to help cut down on shoplifting and robbery in a retail store.

ence of cameras has reduced theft by both shoplifters and employees.

Banks, too, have found that cameras do provide some protection against robberies and passers of bad checks. People who know their pictures are being taken and will be filed away for quick reference if needed tend to think twice before committing a criminal act.

Similarly, photoelectric beams are commonly used by banks, museums, stores, offices, factories, and warehouses. These sensitive optical systems are designed to emit steady beams of light at ranges up to a third of a mile. Anytime the beam of light is interrupted, an alarm signal is set off automatically.

One of the most effective uses of electronic surveillance in recent years has been the employment of "X-ray" machines at airports. These machines, which can "see through" luggage or packages, have been credited with greatly reducing hijacking attempts on airliners.

Widespread use is also being made—both by government agencies and private industry—of a vast array of devices under the general category of perimeter-infusion detection systems. These employ everything from infrared to microwaves to "spot" intruders in secured areas.

Such systems, used for years by the military at camps, bases, arsenals, and storage areas, also have popular application in such areas as airports, prisons, and other institutions of confinement; petroleum refineries; nuclear installations; storage and warehouse operations; railroad facilities; and at marinas, docks, and marine storage sites.

Tiny computer "chips" such as this one now run everything from cameras and refrigerators to Trident ballistic missiles.

Almost all business firms today collect and maintain a considerable amount of personal data on employees. This includes such information as educational background, past employment, past residences, creditors, associations with organizations, religious affiliations, and so forth.

Companies that have defense contracts with the U.S. government or that work on sensitive or classified products or services routinely put prospective employees through thorough field investigations. These may be conducted by such federal agencies as the FBI or by private investigators. The resulting reports often include examinations of academic records, court records, personal credit and litigation, marital status, police records, political affiliation, neighborhood background, past earnings, even personal habits such as drinking, sexual conduct, and moral character.

Almost all of this information now is fed into computers and kept on electronic file. Data is put into the computers as collected, and the full record on any individual can be retrieved in a matter of seconds.

One of the most novel uses of electronic surveillance is being employed in Tokyo, Japan. There, computer "eyes" that can read and identify car license plates and within seconds notify police of a vehicle's location have been installed in streets. These "tell" an overhead television camera of an approaching car. The camera takes still images of the license plates using very fast shutter speeds. Images of the plates are processed and identified by a main computer. They are then collated with a list of "wanted" cars. If a particular car is on the list, the computer tells the time and position of the car to nearby checkpoints manned by police. The entire process takes about six seconds. Japanese authorities say the system is proving to be an effective weapon against car theft.

Such new and innovative uses of electronic surveillance are being found more and more as the technology continues to improve.

CHAPTER 7

PROSPECTING FROM SPACE

Silently, incessantly, unblinking automated sentries peer down upon earth from high-ranging orbital vantage points. Laden with cameras capable of ultrahigh resolution and with sensitive measuring instrumentation, these artificial satellites see and feel the planet's pulse electronically, recording far more than the human eye could possibly see.

One series of these spacecraft is called *Landsat* (for "Land Satellite"). The major purpose of this program, established by the National Aeronautics and Space Administration (NASA) in 1965, with the first satellite launched in 1972, is to survey, inventory, and catalog the earth's natural resources. A secondary purpose is to seek clues that may lead to new supply sources of such precious commodities as oil and rare minerals.

Each *Landsat*—there have been five satellites launched to date—is designed to circle the earth once every 103 minutes, or about 14 times a day, from an orbit 570 miles (912 km) above the planet's surface. The rotation of the earth moves each satellite's track about 1,600 miles (2,560 km) westward along the equator during each orbit. In other words, on one day a *Landsat* will be over Maine during a morning pass, over central Minnesota on its next swing around, over the western por-

—53

tion of Washington state on the next, and so on. The orbital angle is set so that each spacecraft passes over every point under its orbital path every eighteen days. This offers not only broad but repetitive coverage of the earth.

The electronic instrumentation on the Landsat is commonly referred to as its "remote-sensing system." This means that the satellite has the capability of detecting the nature of an object on earth without actually touching it. From space, sensors probe, or "listen to," an object electronically, then convert the electronic signals to a visual record—a photolike image. Remote sensing is made possible by the simple physical fact that any object whose temperature is above absolute zero will reflect, emit, transmit, absorb, or scatter protons, which are the basic units of electromagnetic energy.

Across the visible and invisible spectra, all objects yield distinctive "fingerprints," or spectral signatures, that are determined by the objects' atomic and molecular structures. Signatures not only differentiate objects, they also can indicate size, shape, density, surface texture, moisture content, and other physical and chemical properties.

Wheat, for example, has a different signature from corn or oats. Moreover, identification of these signatures enables scientists to determine not only what an object is, but how old and how healthy it is as well. The cell of a sick plant reflects or emits radiation differently from that of a healthy one.

Human eyes are capable of seeing only a small part of the electromagnetic spectrum. Landsat's eyes, called multispectral scanners, observe the earth in four spectral colors (frequency bands of the spectrum)—two in the visible range and two in the invisible portion of the spectrum beyond the color red, called infrared. These four particular colors were selected to provide the maxi-

This Landsat *photo is of Manhattan in New York.*

mum delineation of certain important features of the earth's surface, such as soil, vegetation, and water, among others.

"False color" techniques are used to enhance the images collected in space. These help investigators to analyze the nature of the subject matter. Green, red, and infrared, seen and recorded separately by the satellites, are combined at NASA's Goddard Space Flight Center in Greenbelt, Maryland. Thus, healthy crops, trees, and other green plants, which are very bright in infrared but invisible to the naked eye, appear as bright red. Suburban areas with sparse vegetation appear as light pink, and barren lands as light gray. Cities and industrial areas show as green or dark gray, and clear water appears black. When the green, red, and infrared are combined in different ways, the image can be analyzed to provide information about the quality, condition, and kinds of objects in the scene in more detail than could be obtained from conventional photography.

As a sort of "bonus" service, data collection systems aboard the spacecraft gather information from unstaffed collection platforms scattered at remote sites throughout the United States and along its coastal regions. These data may include periodic sampling of such local environmental or surface conditions as temperature, humidity, stream flow, and soil moisture.

When the spacecraft is above a transmitting platform and a ground receiving station, the message is relayed immediately to the station through the satellite. Otherwise, the message is stored by onboard tape recorders to be transmitted later. These data are subsequently passed on to individual investigators for detailed analysis.

A data system links the observatory in space with the users on the ground. Information collected by the satellite sensors is converted to electronic signals, processed, and transmitted to earth stations. Here it is received, classified, processed, stored, and/or provided immediately to investigators and other users all over the world.

The Landsat program has been successful beyond even the most optimistic expectations. So prolific is this satellite system that during the first six months of its operation in 1972, Landsat 1 "imaged" nearly 40,000 scenes of the earth's surface. From these, about one and a half million high-quality photographic images were made and sent from NASA to government agencies and investigators for use.

The list of useful kinds of information gleaned from Landsat is enormous. Further, it grows almost daily, as more and more people all around the globe learn how to apply the basic data and the new processing techniques to their own particular needs.

One of the most exciting facets of the Landsat program has been the satellites' capabilities, through processing of the images they take, to locate potential new sources of scarce minerals, oil, and other valuable resources, often in remote regions of the world. By using Landsat images of areas with known petroleum deposits, and correlating these with Landsat images of geologically similar structures elsewhere, geologists are better able to determine where new petroleum deposits may be located.

Landsat is particularly useful in this kind of search because it can show large structural features, such as major fault systems, domes and uplifts, and folded mountain belts of regional or subcontinental size. Petroleum exploration and oil companies use such data to help narrow down their hunt for new sources. One of the greatest benefits of electronic surveillance from space is that potentially productive mineral source areas can be spotted in desolate, barren, or hostile country that would not otherwise be searched, such as the back side of remote mountain ranges, arctic areas, or the middle of vast deserts. For instance, crystal linear features discovered, through *Landsat* images, in the Tanacross area near the Canadian border have led to exploration for previously unknown copper ore deposits.

Landsat has also led to the discovery of rich nickel deposits in western Canada and in South Africa, and to large copper ranges in the isolated outer reaches of Pakistan. Geologists using a new system of enhanced imagery that pinpoints lineaments, anomalies, and structural features with currently known geologic features, were able to predict eleven potential oil drilling locations, and all eleven produced wells.

For agriculture, satellites have the ability to photograph every sizable farm in the world to determine what crop is being raised, tell whether the crop is young or old and healthy or diseased, and accurately predict the yield. Electronic images from space can send advance warnings of droughts, or even the changes in soil condition, to aid the prevention of blight. Other agricultural uses include analysis of soil moisture content, determination of irrigation needs, and timely censuses of livestock.

Experts have used such images to obtain data needed to curb the cotton bollworm in California; to track the dreaded Mediterranean fruit fly on the U.S. west coast; and to survey destruction caused by the Dudaim melon, an inedible variety of cantaloupe that smothers cultivated crops. Mexico has used *Landsat* images to help eradicate the screwworm, which causes annual losses to cattle and poultry in the hundreds of millions of dollars.

In forestry, a satellite electronic sensing system is the only practical way to maintain a constant watch over vast wooded areas to provide warning of insect infestations and diseased trees, take censuses of trees, and report logging yields. In addition, instruments in orbit can spot forest fires burning in places no human has ever seen.

By using *Landsat*, it has been found that timber type identification can be as high as 95 percent accurate and condition identification as high as 80 percent accurate. This contributes significantly to the ability to pinpoint available timber supplies in terms of location, type, quality, and quantity.

In hydrology, satellite imagery is used to inventory water in regional basins by measurement of lake levels, river flow rates, irrigation patterns, and drainage patterns. Satellites also provide early warning of floods by monitoring rainfall and surveying drainage basins. They locate aquifers and determine the suitability of various sites for constructing dams and storing water. And, *Landsat* estimates water resources through snow and frozen water surveys and determines the location of seepage and other ground water sources.

In oceanography, satellites can provide continuous broad-scale surveillance. Infrared instruments in orbit trace the temperature outlines of ocean currents and upwellings and help lead us to one of our major food supplies—fish. Surface temperatures can pinpoint the highest concentrations of plankton, the prime source of food for fish. Such data is relayed to commercial fishing boats all over the world.

Satellite data also is used as a means to monitor such oceanographic features as sea state, distribution of sea ice, surface temperatures, current patterns, and biological development. This provides information vital to the shipping industry.

Landsat satellites also serve as environmental guardians. From space, impartial electronic eyes can see pollution violators, and sensitive instruments can monitor the earth's ecology. From an orbital vantage point, most of the world can be watched continuously and automatically. Pollutants can be detected and identified as they move into water. Violations can be isolated, and ground crews can follow up on the tips from space by taking samples and determining the causes of the violations.

Satellites can also track air pollution and its distribution patterns over great distances. Concentration levels can be identified, as can the rates of movement and dispersion. Such information can be used to tell how far smog or other gases will travel. Pollution alerts, like the storm warnings made possible by weather satellites, can be made in advance.

Continuous observations from space are proving a great boon to land managers and conservationists, too. The U.S. Department of the Interior, for example, uses satellite imagery to help administer nearly 500 million acres of national parks, forests, and public lands. Studies of changing features or conditions such as grasslands status and foraging patterns is supported by synoptic observations from orbit. The relaying of timely and reliable information from space on the distribution, health, and vigor of vegetation and the measurements of snow accumulation and glacial movement greatly enhances the work of environmental managers.

Many states use satellite imagery to help in land-use planning and management. In Mississippi, for instance, the photographs from space distinguish entire transportation networks, including highways, interstate systems, primary and secondary road systems, railroads, power lines, and pipelines. Such data is used in a variety of ways, from school district planning of bus routes to improved residential tax assessments.

Landsat is even helping to identify potential geologic hazards. It has led to a new approach in creating earthquake hazard maps. By plotting earthquake epicenters on *Landsat* images on which new fault lines have been identified, the degree of correlation between the earthquakes and surface fractures is better substantiated. Data from space has been used to discover many geological surface features linked with earthquakes, particularly in sparsely populated western states, that experts had not known existed,

Landsat data also is used extensively in such diverse areas as soil evaluation, climate studies, wildlife management, and cartography.

In general, earth-orbital photography provides surveys of large areas and isolated sections that would require a tremendous amount of time if done by conventional means. In some cases it would be extremely difficult or even impossible to make surveys on the ground. One Landsat satellite, however, takes a picture of the earth every twenty-five seconds. Each picture covers an area 115 miles (184 km) square. To do this by aerial photography would cost more than $100,000. To cover the earth, it would cost billions of dollars.

All Landsat images taken from space are available to users, including the general public, at a very reasonable cost. They are available through a national repository and dissemination agency located at Sioux Falls, South Dakota. The repository is managed by the U.S. Geological Survey.

In February 1986, a French satellite called Spot 1 was launched into earth orbit atop an Ariane rocket. It circles the earth fourteen times a day, passing over each specific point of the globe once every twenty-six days. However, by using mirrors, a particular location can be seen from an angle at least twice a week.

On board Spot are two cameras that can show identifiable images as small as a 33-foot (9.9 m) square while covering areas 37 miles (59.2 km) square. By combining images from various angles on different passes, a three-dimensional image can be produced. Spot has been called the "ultimate sky camera," and the satellite's owners say it can be used for oil and mineral exploration, agriculture, forestry, urban planning, military movements, or navigation, among other uses. *Spot's* high-resolution, close-up photos of earth will be available for sale to anyone willing to pay the price.

Thus, through the technological wonder of electronic surveillance equipment placed in space, we now have the means to measure, catalog, and monitor, economically and effectively, the vast resources of the earth.

CHAPTER 8

WORLDWIDE WEATHER WATCH

On September 8, 1900, a massive hurricane whipped across the Gulf of Mexico and came on land at Galveston, Texas. Churned by winds in excess of 125 miles per hour (140 kmph), the ferocious storm leveled buildings and angry seas flooded the city, creating widespread panic and devastation. In what has been described as the worst natural disaster in the history of the United States, more than 12,000 people lost their lives in that hurricane, 6,000 in Galveston alone.

Such an occurrence could not be repeated today, no matter how strong the storm, thanks to the all-seeing electronic eyes of meteorological satellites in space. Today, residents of endangered areas are warned of the approach of violent weather days in advance, giving them ample time to prepare and, if necessary, evacuate.

For well over a quarter of a century now, sensors operating aboard satellites in earth orbit have been providing a daily weather watch on the world. Today, the thousands of crystal-clear photographs they transmit are all but taken for granted. Yet each year thousands of human lives and billions of dollars in property are saved because of advance warnings of tornadoes, hurricanes, floods, and other storms.

The first weather satellites were called *Tiros* (Television and Infrared Observation Satellite). Launched in the 1960s, they pioneered a new era in meteorological observations and forecasting. One of the most important contributions of the *Tiros* program was development of a revolutionary new camera system, the Automatic Picture Transmission, or APT. When used with relatively inexpensive ground receiving equipment, APT led to the general use of space data from satellites in the preparation of local weather forecasts all over the world. Today, thousands of weather stations worldwide have their own receivers and thus immediate access to the most up-to-the-minute weather information direct from satellites.

By the 1970s, a new, "second generation" series of spacecraft took over the weather watch from space. These were Improved Tiros Operations Satellites (*ITOS*), which offered, for the first time, twenty-four-hour coverage of the earth on a routine basis. Cloud cover pictures at night were made possible by a new scanning infrared radiometer. Infrared has become one of the weather forecaster's most valuable tools. Infrared sensing instruments in satellites can pinpoint the temperatures of the land, sea, and cloudtops to an accuracy of within 3 degrees Fahrenheit.

On the *ITOS* spacecraft, for example, an attitude-control system keeps the specialized instruments continually pointed at earth. Each satellite photographs a strip of clouds about 1,700 miles (2,720 km) wide and 25,000 miles (40,000 km) long every two hours. And each picture taken by the television camera systems covers an approximate 2,000 square miles (5,200 sq. km), or about 4 million square miles (10.36 m. sq. km) of cloud cover. Without satellites, less than 20 percent of the earth's atmosphere can be efficiently observed by conventional meteorological systems.

The Tiros VIII *meteorological satellite*

As advanced as the *ITOS* system was, however, it had one critical shortcoming. Although these satellites covered the entire globe daily, it took a full twelve hours for the spacecraft to get back to the same spot again. This did not provide continuous observations of all points on the earth. Therefore, severe weather, such as thunderstorms or tornadoes, could develop in an area after an *ITOS* pass and cause widespread damage with little or no warning from space. This led to development of the Synchronous Meteorological Satellite (*SMS*) program, which was designed to keep significant portions of the earth's cloud cover under constant surveillance.

SMS satellites have an environmental data collection system that receives information from thousands of sensing platforms placed at remote sites on land, in ships, and in buoys at sea, in rivers, and in lakes. From space, the satellites interrogate these sites, gathering such information as amounts of rainfall, river and stream heights, wind conditions, air temperature, sea state, and even earthquake measurements and volcanic disturbances. Pertinent data is then relayed from space to small regional warning and forecast stations around the world.

Today's weather satellites also measure the speed of the wind, the temperature of the air, and the amount of moisture in it. All of this information helps meteorologists predict everyday weather as well as spot dangerous and unusual weather systems such as hurricanes. Even the amount of rain a hurricane will bring can now be accurately forecast. Temperature monitoring further makes it possible to predict freezes far enough ahead so that farmers can prepare for them. Because weather satellites have sensors that can feel and measure heat and the amount of smoke and chemicals in the air, they can also help monitor pollution over cities and large industrial areas.

In the late 1970s, the Synchronous Meteorological Satellite program changed names and became known as GOES—Geostationary Operational Environmental Satellite. A fleet of GOES and other satellites—some hovering at fixed points above the equator, others in polar orbits (traveling from pole to pole)—provides not only an almost continuous view of weather patterns all over the globe but also a flood of other data including vegetation cover on land, oceanic and atmospheric temperatures, and particle activity surrounding the earth. These spacecraft are complemented by a number of similar foreign satellites. In fact, more than 120 nations depend on satellites for daily meteorological data.

Currently circling the earth in polar orbit, about 500 miles (800 km) up, are two NOAA (National Oceanic and Atmospheric Administration) satellites. Each covers the entire earth twice a day. They are the latest in a long line of spacecraft that are providing advanced imagery data and special radiation measurements from which vertical "profiles" of temperature and water vapor content can be calculated. About 16,000 global soundings are provided daily by these satellites, adding valuable information about weather conditions over ocean areas, where conventional data is lacking.

Higher up, the geosynchronous GOES satellites, from altitudes of about 22,240 miles (35,584 km) above earth, provide full-earth-disc pictures every 30 minutes throughout the day and night. Presently, GOES 5 monitors North and South America and most of the Atlantic Ocean. GOES 6 covers North America and much of the Pacific Ocean basin. Collectively, their capabilities permit near-continuous viewing of storms and cloud cover, as well as determination of wind fields at cloud altitudes. In addition, GOES satellites are used to send satellite imagery and weather maps to amateur and professional users.

These newer generations of spacecraft and instruments have increased and enhanced the number, type, and value of meteorological observations and applications. They have also proven useful in other areas, ranging from the detection of volcanic eruptions to the assessment of agricultural and oceanic conditions.

Here are some specific areas where electronic meteorological surveillance from space is helping to improve life on earth:

STORM WARNINGS AND WEATHER FORECASTS—Since the startup of a U.S. operational satellite service in February 1966, no tropical storm has gone undetected anywhere in the world. Satellites are particularly good at detecting and tracking tropical cyclones, hurricanes, and typhoons. Early warnings made possible by such advance notice have saved thousands of human lives and billions of dollars in property damage.

From their permanent geosynchronous vantage points, satellites also can provide near-continuous coverage of the atmospheric environment that breeds tornadoes, squall lines, and local severe thunderstorms. Sophisticated imagery can even detect the "ingredients" of a storm before it develops. Additionally, *GOES* imagery is used to estimate rainfall amounts for flash flood warnings. In winter, polar-orbiting spacecraft keep watch on mountain snowpacks and river ice jams to warn of potential spring melt flooding.

As to forecasting improvements, the American Meteorological Society in 1983 said that weather satellites "have contributed significantly to the increase in accuracy achieved over the past twenty-five years in daily weather forecasting for periods of one to five days."

ICE AND SNOW—Satellites have greatly improved global mapping of sea and lake ice, and they monitor seasonal variations of the polar icecap. Such information helps keep ships from being trapped by sea-ice formations in the Arctic area. This is especially helpful to such operations as offshore oil exploration and Great Lakes shipping, and as a navigational aid.

FIRE AND SMOKE—Volcanic eruption, such as at Mt. St. Helens in 1980, can be instantly spotted and followed via space surveillance, and quick warnings can be dispatched to anyone in danger areas. Further, a special infrared channel on polar-orbiting satellite sensors is particularly sensitive to high heat sources. It has proven effective in pinpointing wild fires in remote areas. Large-scale fires and the smoke they generate are also detectable in visible imagery by both types of weather satellites.

VEGETATION—*GOES* satellite images are used to monitor the southward progress of freezing surface temperatures, so warnings can be given to fruit farmers. Polar-orbiting spacecraft carry sensors sensitive to chlorophyll—the "green" in plants. This capability is used to survey crops and vegetation to determine their density and vigor, and may alert those on the ground to possible conditions of drought and deforestation.

SEA SURFACE TEMPERATURE AND OCEAN CURRENTS—Sea surface temperature observations from space help meteorologists study ocean influences on weather and climate, and can be useful in helping to predict heavy rains and flooding. Such surface analyses also have proven of great value to the fishing industry by finding schools of tuna, salmon, and swordfish.

Despite all these advantages, experts say we have only begun to tap the full potential of electronic surveillance and weather satellites. Even today, NOAA scientists are searching satellite imagery for new clues to environmental dynamics and new applications for the vast amounts of data being transmitted from space to earth.

The United States is being joined in this worldwide weather watch by many other nations. Japan has a geostationary meteorological satellite over the Western Pacific Ocean. The European Space Agency's *Meteosat* monitors Europe, Africa, the Mediterranean, and the eastern Atlantic. India's *Insat* observes the Indian Ocean and surrounding regions, and the Soviet Union operates two polar-orbiting spacecraft.

Before we had satellites and electronic surveillance systems, weather observations covered less than one fifth of the globe. Little if any information was available for the polar regions or vast stretches of Asia, Africa, and South America. Ships at sea and islands were at the mercy of great tropical storms, for there was no advance warning of their approach. Today, however, weather satellites provide practically continuous viewing and remote sensing of the atmosphere on a global scale, benefiting us all.

CHAPTER 9
THE NEW MILITARY HIGH GROUND

In May 1960 a tall, young pilot, wearing a regulation flying suit and helmet but with no markings, strode across the runway at a remote airstrip in what was then Peshawar, West Pakistan. Strapped to his hip was a revolver. Deftly, he climbed into the cockpit of a strange-looking low black jet plane with a high tail. It looked out of place among the rows of shiny military aircraft nearby.

Minutes later he was soaring into the sky on what was announced as a routine high-altitude weather research flight. Steadily, the sleek plane climbed, past the ceiling of transports, beyond the point at which military planes fly, and then above the reach of any other known aircraft. He leveled off at an altitude above 60,000 feet—nearly 12 miles (19.2 km) up.

The pilot's name was Francis Gary Powers, and he was not logging meteorological data. He was, instead, on a secret mission. He was to fly past the Ural Mountains across Russia to Murmansk and then land at another base in Bodo, Norway. Powers' real assignment was to spy on military installations deep within the Soviet Union.

His advanced U-2 aircraft was loaded with super-sophisticated electronic equipment that included high-resolution, infrared cameras that could pinpoint an object as small as a tank even from this lofty height. Other gear was designed to sample the atmosphere for radioactive evidence of illegal nuclear tests.

It was believed, by Powers and U.S. military officials, that the U-2 could fly not only out of the range of anti-aircraft fire but even above the detection capabilities of Russian radar. It thus came as a considerable shock to the pilot when he discovered that midway across the vast Soviet frontier, his plane had been hit by anti-aircraft fire and was obviously going to crash. Powers had the means to take his own life but chose not to. Instead, he parachuted to the ground, where both he and the remnants of his plane were captured.

Exploiting his incident to the fullest, the Russians, brandishing the proof, told the story of the U.S. spy flights to the world. It hit with dramatic impact and greatly embarrassed the United States.

As it turned out, the United States had been flying such secret missions for more than four years, a fact that the State Department admitted in a subsequent news briefing. A spokesman, Lincoln White, said at the time, "The necessity for such activities as measures for legitimate national defense is enhanced by the excessive secrecy practiced by the Soviet Union in contrast to the free world."

The Eisenhower administration pronounced that such flights were essential because the United States had no other way to gather important intelligence information on which to build its own defensive forces. This was the dawn of the intercontinental ballistic missile age, and the United States deemed it vital to know what kind of missiles the Russians were building and stockpiling, and where. Without such knowledge, claimed military experts, the United States could not properly defend itself against possible enemy attack.

Gary Powers standing in front of a model of his spy plane, a U-2 aircraft

Such measures were, of course, by no means new. Military spying is as old as war itself. Perhaps one of the first uses of electronic surveillance in the area of spying occurred more than 120 years ago when, during the U.S. Civil War, Union General George McClellan used a tethered balloon to survey the defense of Richmond, Virginia, with a "crude" new device known as the camera.

Although some may say that any manner of spying is despicable, proponents counter that using whatever means are available to keep tabs on the enemy helps prevent wars, or, at the least, helps us prepare for them.

The Cuban missile crisis of 1962 is an example. For months, the United States suspected the Soviet Union of supplying Cuba with deadly missile components, a situation that was untenable to U.S. military defenses since the island is only 90 miles (144 km) from the United States.

To verify these suspicions, President John F. Kennedy authorized high-altitude U-2 aircraft flights over Cuba. The resulting photos showed clearly that not only was Russia supplying Cuba with missiles, but its technicians were helping install them at strategic sites.

In October 1962, Kennedy ordered the famous blockade of Russian ships steaming toward Cuba. For a few harrowing days, the world seemed on the brink of another world war. But finally, Soviet Premier Nikita Khrushchev ordered his ships to turn around and return home, and the Cuban missile bases were dismantled.

It was a natural progression to go from spying using aircraft in the earth's atmosphere to putting spy satellites in space. And, again, these provide a useful and necessary service. Orbiting reconnaissance and nuclear-detection satellites tend to keep the world's major powers "honest." By providing an up-to-the-minute strategic weapons inventory, they allay fears by eliminating unknowns and actually can contribute meaningfully to international arms-control agreements, which probably would be impossible without them.

An aerial photograph of the San Cristobal area in Cuba, where a missile base was being constructed

"We have space-based systems for reconnaissance, early warning [of missile or other attacks], communications, charting, meteorology, and geodesy," says Grant Hansen, former assistant secretary of the U.S. Air Force for research and development.

"These systems do not pose a threat to the security of other nations," Hansen says. "They are used to provide information that enhances our deterrent capability, not to carry weapons that might be used offensively."

Hansen describes some of the distinct advantages of using space for such military purposes: "Because of the tremendous area of earth coverage from a satellite, its capabilities are highly superior for data gathering functions requiring broad coverage, such as cloud cover and meteorology, earth resources surveillance over land and water, communications relay, and detection of missile launches.

"Space is uniquely capable of wide area coverage for detecting and characterizing missile launches. Satellites viewing a tremendous volume of near-earth space without atmospheric interference provide a unique capability for nuclear burst detection, to monitor treaty compliance, and for solar radiation data gathering to predict radio communications performance."

Military officials contend that the importance of maintaining an integrated ground-airborne-spaceborne intelligence-gathering network is that, despite the Soviet Union's vast and growing arsenal of nuclear missiles, emplaced only thirty minutes from American cities, the Defense Department is fairly confident that a surprise attack like that at Pearl Harbor in December 1941 is now almost impossible.

Actually, military communications satellites fulfill strategic as well as tactical missions. Strategic missions tie satellites to a group of fixed earth stations; hence, communications can be established over any path on which two or more stations are mutually "visible" to or-

NORAD, deep within the Cheyenne Mountain in Colorado, is the command center for the screening of potential enemy missile attacks. NORAD commanders are constantly scanning the skies over North America and, thanks to high-speed computers, have at their fingertips an enormous amount of real-time information on their own and foreign defense systems.

biting spacecraft. The tactical system permits communications between the satellite and a variety of earth stations that may include mobile ones such as those in aircraft, ships, automobiles, or even properly equipped infantrymen.

During the Vietnam War, for example, satellites regularly transmitted high-speed digital data from South Vietnam to Washington. Within minutes after processing, high-quality reconnaissance photographs of battle zones were available to Pentagon analysts via the Defense Department's Initial Defense Satellite Communications System. The revolutionary impact on strategic planning is obvious.

Today, dozens of U.S. military satellites ring the earth at all times. The exact number of them used strictly for spying purposes remains top secret, as is most information about how they perform. What is known, however, is that many of these satellites are in north-south polar orbits, routes that enable them to pass over each part of the globe every few hours.

Closest to earth are photo-reconnaissance satellites, which can zoom in to about 100 miles (160 km) over the Soviet Union or any other place on earth. These early-warning spacecraft serve two complementary missions. One takes panoramic photographs from earth orbit to detect evidence of new construction and installations of military interest such as airfields, missile sites, and strategic targets. The second is a "close-look" satellite used to obtain high-resolution photos of specific installations.

The U.S. Air Force's *Big Bird* spacecraft, for instance, keeps watch over a large number of Russian military installations. Its cameras can be programmed from earth stations to zoom in and out, photographing wide fields of view or moving in so close that a trained photographic interpreter will be able to identify individual vehicles on the ground. The most recent developments include phased-array radars that can detect objects the size of a basketball from as far as 600 miles (960 km) up in orbit.

Big Bird has the remarkable ability to photograph all of the Soviet Union and the People's Republic of China every three and a half days. It and other satellites carry a variety of cameras. When the film has been exposed, it is automatically placed in canisters that are then parachuted back to earth, where they are either snagged by planes in mid-air or retrieved from the ocean by divers. Once developed, the images are projected on screens and analyzed by photo intelligence specialists who can magnify objects of particular interest with computerized lenses, or process the photos to reveal details hidden to the human eye.

Another type of satellite, known as *KH-11*, uses no film at all. Instead, it records elements of a scene as digital electronic impulses that can be transmitted to other satellites and then to ground stations almost instantaneously. Although the *KH-11*'s resolution is not as good as that of the other reconnaissance satellites, the advantage of direct transmission is that it enables officials to obtain important images without delay.

New generations of reconnaissance satellites, now under development, soon will be able to swoop from high altitudes to as close as 75 miles (120 km) for looks at "suspicious" areas. They will enable the United States not only to keep track of every ship at sea, but to monitor the movements of all aircraft as well. Besides giving early warning of an enemy missile attack, these satellites could also follow the movement of military transport planes.

A new series of *Navstar* navigation satellites soon will add a nuclear detonation detection system to their orbital payloads. Such a system, encompassing twenty-one satellites ringing the earth, will include X-ray, optical, and electromagnetic-pulse sensors. Its computers will analyze the data gathered to pinpoint the location of a nuclear detonation to within a mile (1.6 km). Data will be transmitted to the ground as it is received, so a bomb blast will be detected and acted upon almost immediately.

Nearly half the spy satellites are in geosynchronous orbit, at an altitude of 23,500 miles (37,600 km). Each is stationary, remaining above a point on the equator, moving at the same speed as the earth's rotation.

These are called "staring" satellites because they keep a single area under constant surveillance rather than circling the earth. Most of them are used for early warning of the launch of ballistic missiles and for communications.

If, for example, Russia fired a missile from a launch pad deep inside the Soviet interior, a U.S. infrared satellite in stationary orbit would immediately detect its exhaust trail. The relayed data from space would tell experts instantly how many missiles were fired and in what direction each is heading.

The Satellite Early Warning System (*SEWS*) detects over 500 missile launches annually, and spacecraft instrumentation is sensitive enough to detect missiles that are much smaller than intercontinental ballistic missiles. It can also pick up nuclear explosions, which release infrared energy. Currently, one of these satellites is stationed over the Indian Ocean, one over Brazil, and one over the Pacific Ocean, providing continuous coverage of the Soviet Union, China, and the United States.

More sensitive than *SEWS* is a new system called *Teal Ruby,* which tracks from orbit the flight paths of aircraft and missiles by means of an array of infrared detectors that concentrate on a specific area of the earth. *SEWS* sensors focus on an object and lock onto it while the satellite continues orbiting.

Today, certain world events might happen too rapidly for any of these satellites to be swung into position. If that happens, the military relies on a proven resource—the spy plane.

The fastest such plane, known as an SR-71, or *Blackbird*, can reportedly fly at more than 2,000 miles per hour (3,200 kmph) at altitudes of up to 85,000 feet (255,000 m). *Blackbird*'s cameras can film 100,000 square miles (260,000 sq. km) in an hour. An area the size of the entire United States could be covered in three passes. And the photography can be pinpointed to produce three-dimensional images of a 150-square-mile (442.5-sq.-km) area that are so sharp a mailbox can be distinguished on a country road.

Aside from these impressive "eyes" in space, the United States also has matching sets of electronic "ears"—sensors designed to listen, not observe. Indeed, a wide variety of sensitive sound-detection instruments are implanted aboard satellites, aircraft, ships, and submarines, as well as ground stations positioned all over the world.

One set of satellites, so called "ferrets," monitor radio and radar signals from geosynchronous orbits in space. They pick up and send back to earth everything from the radio traffic of foreign military units on the move to the private communications of foreign leaders. These and other devices intercept not only telephone traffic but also radio, microwave, and satellite communications, as well as radar and telemetry data from missile tests.

Rhyolite satellites intercept data transmitted from Soviet missiles in flight. From geosynchronous orbits, each of these spacecraft consists of a huge radio "ear" turned to earth, banks of solar cells to provide power, and a transmitter to send signals back to the ground. It can intercept radio communications across all bands and can simultaneously transmit 11,000 two-way telephone conversations.

A different type of listening satellite, called *Shite*

The reconnaissance aircraft known as Blackbird

Cloud, can intercept Soviet submarine and ship communications, and yet another satellite orbits at a lower altitude and is designed expressly to monitor Soviet and Chinese military radar transmissions.

These spacecraft are supplemented by several other eavesdropping systems, ranging from a fleet of older U-2 spy planes and SR-71 aircraft to the larger RC-135 series of planes. It was from data received aboard an RC-135 that the United States learned that the Russians had shot down a Korean airliner in 1983.

The aircraft and spacecraft, in turn, are backed by a sophisticated system of ground-based radar and antennas throughout the world. The most important of these is "Cobra Dane," a huge radar installation on Shemya Island, located off Alaska, only 500 miles (800 km) from Russia's Kamchatka Peninsula. It can detect an object the size of a basketball at a range of 2,000 miles (3,200 km).

Cobra Dane scans the skies electronically with over 34,000 radar "eyes" able to track as many as 300 missiles as they speed through the earth's atmosphere; it can track another 200 objects in space. It sweeps the skies by constantly switching electronic impulses in every magnitude and direction.

A similar radar system, "Cobra Judy," positioned aboard the ship *U.S.N.S. Observation Island,* constantly sails about the Pacific Ocean. The two systems together enable the United States to detect and simultaneously track over 500 objects. In addition, there is a worldwide network of ground-based antennas tuned into the secret conversations of Soviet leaders and military officials.

One other form of monitoring, vital to the detection of nuclear blasts, especially underground ones, is performed by seismometers. Composed of magnets fixed to the ground and sensitive spring devices attached to electric coils, seismometers can be placed anywhere in arrays and can sense distant earth tremors and distinguish them from earthquakes.

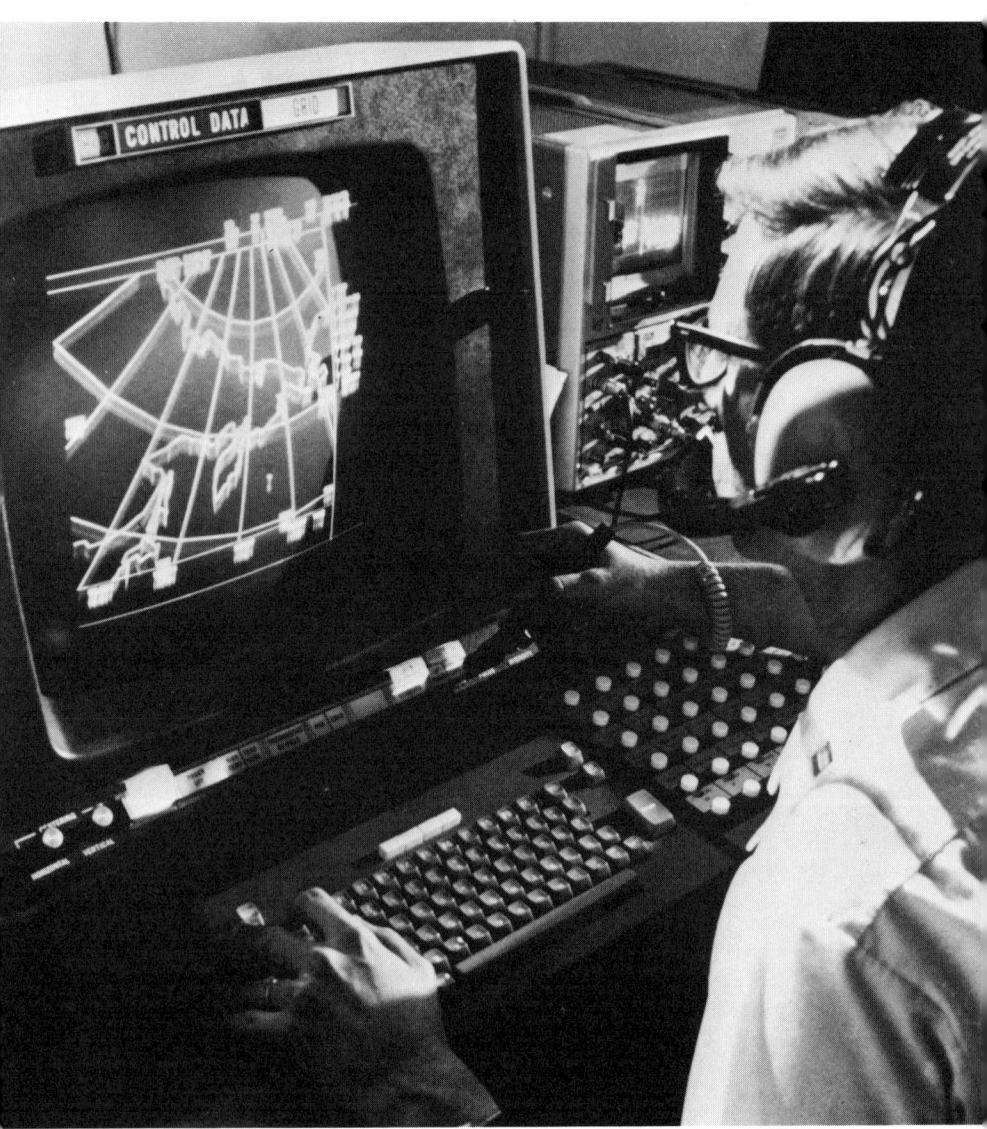

The profile of a missile shows on this control room display within the Cobra Dane radar complex. An Air Force specialist tracks its flight.

One example of how these electronic eyes and ears work together, in space and on earth, occurred during the launch and flight of a Russian SS-25 missile in 1983. When the missile was sighted on its pad by orbiting cameras, sensors listened for the countdown. Once the missile rose above the clouds, the heat of its engine was detected by a U.S. early warning satellite. Broadcasts of its in-flight signals were picked up by satellites. At the same time, the flight itself was observed by powerful radars.

Summing up the overall U.S. spying capabilities, Admiral Stansfield Turner, a former director of the CIA, says, "We can take detailed photographs from very long distances, detect heat sources through infrared devices, pinpoint metal with magnetic detectors, distinguish between barely moving and stationary objects through the use of Doppler radar, use radar to detect objects that are covered or hidden by darkness, eavesdrop on all manner of signals from the human voice to electronic radio waves, detect nuclear radiation with refined Geiger counters, and sense underground explosions at long distances with seismic devices."

All of this, say military officials, helps deter war. As arms control expert Jeffrey Smith points out, "Nations that know their enemies are observing them are far less likely to threaten international peace through rash behavior. Governments also are more likely to propose and sign treaties if they believe they can verify their enemies' compliance with the treaty terms. Also, if a foreign power knows that it cannot initiate a major attack on another nation without immediate detection and therefore chance the launch of a retaliatory strike in kind, it is far less likely to take aggressive action."

In this very practical sense, the vast arsenal of electronic eyes and ears on the ground, in the air, and circling high overhead in space, are performing a vital daily mission that helps keep peace on earth.

CHAPTER 10

TOWARD A POLICE STATE

Technology, it has often been said, is a two-edged sword. When it is applied for its intended useful services, it is very good. But when it is misused, it can be very bad. This is one of the major problems we face today as the refining of electronic surveillance devices and systems marches on.

As we have seen in the preceding chapters, when properly used, such surveillance offers great benefits for a wide variety of meaningful purposes. But as we shall now learn, illegal applications can prove harmful in a number of ways.

One of the best known misuses of electronic surveillance was described in the opening chapter of this book—the bugging of the Democratic National Party campaign headquarters in Washington, D.C., in June 1972. But actually, abuses are almost as old as the systems themselves.

Samuel F. B. Morse invented the telegraph in 1837, and wiretapping probably followed soon after. California passed a law against wiretapping in 1862, and arrests were made in that state two years later when tappers were discovered intercepting and then selling news of stock operations on the East Coast. During the Civil War, soldiers were trained to tap telegraph wires to gather enemy military intelligence data.

In a famous case in 1916, the mayor of New York City authorized police to tap the telephone conversations of five Catholic priests to obtain evidence in an investigation of charity frauds. When the *New York Times* reported not only this story but the fact that police had been wiretapping since 1895, it caused a public uproar. Interestingly, the *Times* supported the police and in an editorial said: "[We] feel too few wires have been tapped, not too many, and that the expose has hurt the cause of justice."

In 1940, as World War II was approaching, President Franklin D. Roosevelt issued an executive order authorizing the attorney general to use "listening devices." The Justice Department interpreted this as an okay to conduct microphone surveillance as well as telephone wiretapping in "national security cases."

In fact, it has been under the "cloak" of national security that several federal government agencies have conducted illegal electronic surveillance on a widespread basis. And, as has only been disclosed in recent years, a great number of these instances had nothing to do with national security. Many, such as the Watergate case, involved politics.

David Wise, author of the book *The American Police State,* says the techniques used by the government against the people have included wiretapping, bugging, break-ins, the opening of mail, cable interception, and physical surveillance. Among the chief users of such techniques over the years have been the Federal Bureau of Investigation, the Central Intelligence Agency, the Internal Revenue Service, and the White House itself.

The FBI, for example, has collected domestic intelligence about individual citizens and groups for half a century, using wiretapping, bugging, clandestine photographic surveillance, and other techniques. For most of that time, both the general public and the U.S. Congress knew little about such activities, or assumed that the FBI had the right to do it. However, for the most part, this was not true. The majority of the FBI's electronic surveillance has been illegal.

As early as 1951, the late FBI director J. Edgar Hoover told then-Attorney General Howard McGrath that his agency had used microphones "for intelligence purposes." He also admitted that in a number of instances it had not been possible to install bugs without trespassing, a clear violation of the law.

Frank Donner, a Yale Law School professor and FBI expert, writing in the magazine *The Nation* in 1974, called the FBI "a secret police force [that] has spied into and kept records on the lives of Americans without authority from either Congress or the Executive [the president]."

Perhaps the best known abuse of electronic surveillance practiced by the FBI was in its long-standing coverage of the late civil rights leader Martin Luther King, Jr. King was under almost continuous surveillance from the late 1950s until his death in 1968. Wherever King and his entourage traveled, it seemed, the FBI followed, wiretapping and bugging his offices and hotel rooms.

Hoover claimed this was necessary for national security because he believed King was surrounded and influenced by communist agents. However, it was revealed

Above: *J. Edgar Hoover.*
Below: *Martin Luther King, Jr. (at microphone) in front of the United Nations after leading a parade to protest the war in Vietnam*

later that Hoover had a personal vendetta against King and tried everything in his power to discredit him.

In 1964, during the Democratic National Convention in Atlantic City, President Lyndon Johnson had King's hotel rooms bugged. The FBI later said it did so because there was fear of "strife and violence" at the convention. But the actual purpose was to learn what King and others might do to further their civil rights cause. Johnson did not want to be embarrassed at the convention.

Hoover was also known to use various means of surveillance, including electronic, to gather surreptitious files on members of Congress, other government officials, and celebrities. On occasion, he shared his ill-gained gossip with President Johnson and others.

In the late 1960s and early 1970s, when there were student protests against the Vietnam War, the FBI actively bugged and wiretapped students and organizations on campuses across the country. All of this activity was illegal. It came to light in 1971 when files were stolen from an FBI office in Media, Pennsylvania, and made public through news reports. The documents proved that the agency snooped on college campuses and in black neighborhoods and harassed innocent citizens and groups.

Such actions prompted former U.S. Senator Edward Long to comment in 1966: "The Justice Department's use of wiretapping and its double standard of enforcement, running from lukewarm efforts against private wiretappers to none at all against law-enforcement wiretappers, has had a disastrous effect on privacy in the United States. Congress and the Supreme Court have done little enough in this area, but even this little has been mostly done by the attitude of the Justice Department."

Some years later, William Sullivan, long a top FBI official under Hoover, told a Senate intelligence committee, "... never once did I hear anybody, including myself, raise the question 'Is this course of action which we have agreed upon lawful, is it legal, is it ethical or moral?' "

The Central Intelligence Agency was created in 1947, and its charter decreed that it have responsibility for intelligence gathering only outside the United States. But it soon began clandestine operations within the country. Like the FBI, the CIA has a long history of electronic surveillance.

In 1974, the *New York Times* ran a major article that said the CIA had conducted "a massive illegal domestic intelligence operation" against political dissidents, secretly compiling files on thousands of American citizens, conducting break-ins, tapping wires, and opening mail. After initial denials, the agency later admitted in congressional testimony that the article was essentially true.

A year later, a special commission headed by former U.S. Vice President Nelson Rockefeller spent months investigating CIA activities in the United States and issued a 300-page report. It accused the CIA of gathering information about the Vietnam War peace movement by using such techniques as physical surveillance, wiretapping, bugging, and break-ins. The report stated, "The unauthorized entries into the homes and offices of American citizens were illegal."

The commission cited one case where the CIA spied on one of its own employees who had attended a meeting of an organization suspected of "foreign ties." CIA agents entered the employee's apartment and cut through walls from an adjacent room to install seven microphones. Through these, conversations in every room of the apartment could be overheard.

Further, it was disclosed that the CIA offered courses to local police in such subjects as covert photography, surveillance, and bugging. Such schooling was allegedly discontinued in the aftermath of the Watergate debacle.

Another agency that reportedly has conducted

classes, specifically in wiretapping, is the Internal Revenue Service, the tax-collecting arm of the U.S. Treasury Department. Bugging, lock picking, the use of amplifiers and recorders, ultraviolet light, and photography were also taught in the department's "Technical Investigative Aids School."

IRS use of electronic surveillance apparently goes back more than thirty years. In 1954, for instance, a former government employee named William Mellin disclosed to a Senate committee that in his forty-year career he had tapped in excess of 60,000 pairs of wires. Much of his work was done for the IRS and other government agencies. He said, "After five years of varied experience with the telephone company, including wiretapping, I devoted the rest of my life to the science of wiretapping for local, state, and federal authorities." Another congressional witness, Owen Burke Yung, told of continuous wiretapping and electronic snooping by the IRS from the early 1940s through the mid-1960s. And in 1965, the commissioner of the Internal Revenue Service turned over to a congressional subcommittee a list of twenty-two cities in which the IRS had concealed microphones in its conference rooms, all without the knowledge of those being overheard.

The telephone of Daniel Ellsberg was also tapped in the early 1970s. Ellsberg is the man who gave the *New York Times* access to the famous "Pentagon Papers," which disclosed many government actions in the Vietnam War that had previously been kept secret.

In the fever of this era, when anti-war sentiment was running high, especially on college campuses, the so-called "Huston Plan" was also launched by the Nixon administration. This was a strategy, attributed to a government official named Tom Charles Huston, which called for eavesdropping on intercommunications within the National Security Agency, bugging, wiretapping, and illegal opening of first class mail. The supposed reason for all this law-breaking activity was to learn about the communist influence at colleges and universities.

And, of course, the most publicized case of electronic surveillance misuse during this time was that of the secret tapes Nixon himself made of conversations inside the Oval Office of the White House—tapes that ironically helped force Nixon to resign the presidency in 1974.

These are but a few examples of the many known forms of electronic surveillance abuse that have been practiced by the U.S. government, mostly over the past thirty or forty years. It is probably just the tip of a vast iceberg. For every published misuse, surely there are many more instances that have never come to light. Multiply this by the fifty state governments and the countless county, city, and municipal areas, and the potential for massive spying on Americans becomes truly frightening.

The federal Drug Enforcement Administration, too, has been called on to explain its covert surveillance activities to Congress. It has told of using two-way radios, walkie-talkies, and devices for wiretapping. The DEA maintained that such gear was used only against drug peddlers, hoodlums, frauds, con men, and others. However, David Wise, author of *The American Police State*, has said that "instances have come to light in which the DEA has been caught snooping into the private lives of more responsible citizens."

At times over the past quarter century, the president of the United States and other high-level executive branch officials have themselves ordered electronic spying, again without legal precedence. In the early 1960s, President John F. Kennedy authorized wiretaps in an investigation of sugar lobbying by the Dominican Republic and other countries. Kennedy also reportedly had the hotel room of a U.S. congressman, Harold Cooley of North Carolina, bugged. Cooley at the time was chairman of the House Agriculture Committee.

The Nixon administration, however, made the most sweeping use of electronic surveillance, in many forms. Prior to Watergate, President Nixon and Henry Kissinger, then head of the National Security Agency, became increasingly disturbed by news leaks about the Vietnam War that they felt were coming from high places inside certain government agencies. When the United States secretly bombed Cambodia, for example, this news was smuggled to the media.

In a desperate effort to plug such leaks, the telephones of seventeen government officials and news reporters were illegally tapped. One tap, on national political columnist Joseph Kraft, was in effect for four years.

As author Wise has said, "An American police state has evolved, operating in the shadows side by side with the legitimate system of government. It has emerged in spite of the Bill of Rights and the protections of the law and the Constitution."

And, more than sixty years ago, in 1924, U.S. Attorney General Harlan Fiske Stone warned: "There is always the possibility that a secret police may become a menace to free government and free institutions, because it carries with it the possibility of abuses of power which are not always quickly apprehended or understood.... When a police system passes beyond these limits, it is dangerous to the proper administration of justice and to human liberty, which it should be our first concern to cherish."

CHAPTER 11
INDUSTRIAL ESPIONAGE

Several years ago Schenley Industries, a company that sold alcoholic beverages, among other things, was working on some confidential plans for future projects. Since their industry was a highly competitive one, many precautions were taken to protect the plans' secrecy.

Despite these efforts, however, word of Schenley's activities mysteriously began surfacing in business circles. Suspicious, the company's president called in an electronics expert. In the study of the executive's home in Florida, a small transmitter was found concealed in the bar. Further, a wiretap was discovered on the lines leading to the president's private office telephone. It had been converted into a microphone that picked up everything said in his office.

The Schenley case was not uncommon. In the fiercely competitive world of business and industry, electronic snooping and espionage are common weapons. More recently, in the early 1980s, a number of experts were found tapping, bugging, and using other surveillance techniques in the high technology computer chip industry. Many of these surfaced in "Silicon Valley" in California, where a large number of these firms are located.

In 1982, Douglas Southard, a deputy district attorney

in Santa Clara County, California, said, "In the past five years probably $100 million or more in electronic technology and products has been stolen in this county area alone." Many companies refuse to publicly discuss thefts or report them to authorities, so Southard's figure may have represented only a small part of the problem.

In electronics and other fast-moving businesses, where new inventions are the order of the day, some unscrupulous business people will use any means they can to learn what their competitors are up to. In fact, industrial spying is often as shadowy and intriguing as espionage is during war.

And it is surprisingly widespread. In 1962, a trade magazine, *Industrial Research,* conducted a survey of such practices. They polled dozens of business firms, and nearly every one of them considered wiretapping a dangerous activity that was not ethically right or legal. Yet, amazingly, a third of the companies using electronic surveillance equipment reported that they either tapped phones themselves or hired someone to do it for them. Another third refused to say whether they wiretapped or not, or used other forms of clandestine surveillance.

Shockingly, the survey revealed that more than half of the larger firms queried were involved in some form of corporate snooping. In other words, they carried on formal programs of espionage.

Above: *this listening device, installed inside a tape dispenser, was used for industrial espionage. Below: the Japanese firm Cony shows off one of its newest "bug detector" devices to help combat industrial espionage.*

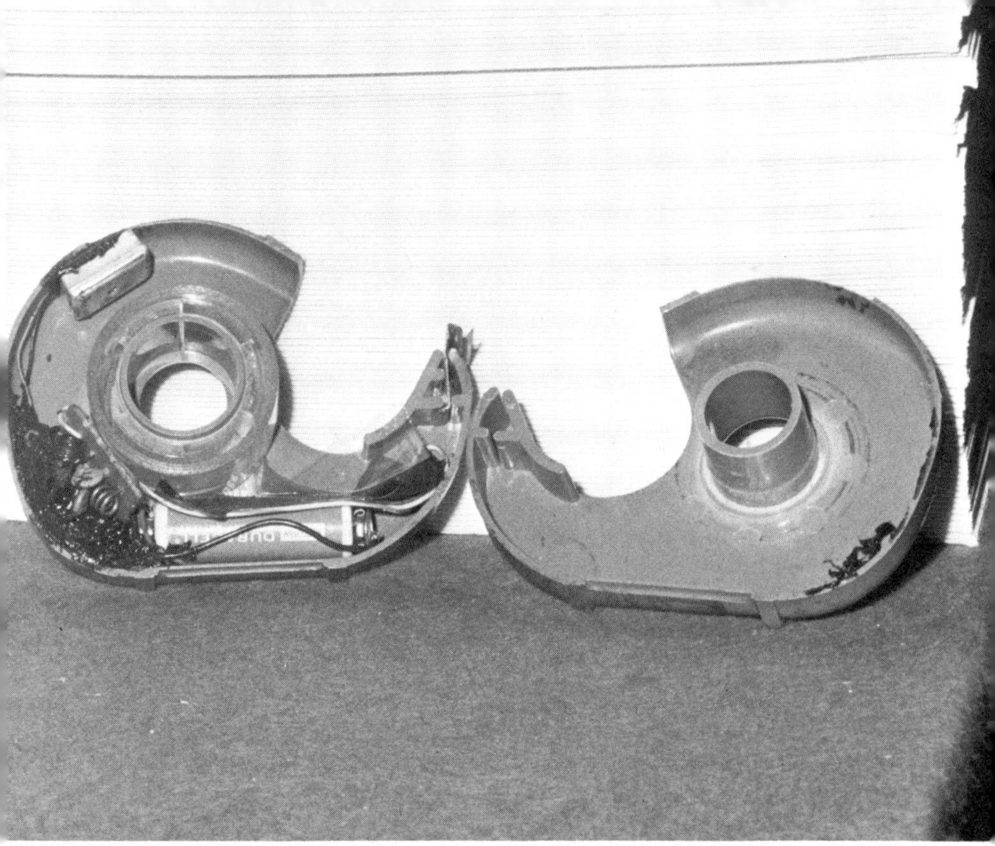

But this is only one form of electronic surveillance abuse found in the private sector. There are many others. Many stores throughout the nation are today routinely equipped with closed-circuit television cameras, for example. Their stated intended purpose is to curtail theft. However, labor leaders have charged that many businesses use them to secretly spy on employees, to see if they are working or goofing off on the job.

Some stores, including Macy's department store in New York City, have at times installed wiretaps on their own phones. Officials have said this was done in an effort to catch employees stealing merchandise. But critics have contended this represents illegal spying on workers, who are unaware that their telephone conversations are being monitored.

In one instance in a factory in Cleveland, Ohio, company management had the women's washroom bugged and rigged to a speaker in the front office. The purpose here was not to catch thieves but rather to overhear gossip about a forthcoming union election.

The range of business abuses sometimes stretches the imagination. A California investigating committee once uncovered several used car dealers in the state who had installed secret microphones in their sales offices. They would then leave prospective car buyers alone in the office to discuss what they were willing to pay for the car. The dealers and their sales staff, listening to this private information, then knew exactly how high they could go with their price offer.

Another form of abuse is through the seeing or turning over of employee records to firms who could use the information for credit ratings, sales pitches, or whatever. Such information should be considered confidential but is often given out in return for money or other favors.

In recent years, in this age of computerized record keeping, many respectable companies have taken steps to protect the privacy of their workers. IBM, the Bank of

America, and the Equitable Life Assurance Company, for example, take strong stands about the safeguarding and proper use of records, and release them only to legal requestors, such as government agencies. Equitable considers personal information collected and maintained "to be of a confidential nature, recognizing our responsibility to provide adequate safeguards to maintain that confidentiality."

There are also many private misuses of electronic surveillance. Bugs, wiretaps, and cameras are among the favorite tools of private investigators, many of whom openly admit they use them regularly in divorce and custody cases. If a woman suspects her husband of "cheating" on her, for instance, she may hire an investigator. The investigator then may plant illegal bugs in hotel rooms or tap the husband's telephone calls or photograph him, even in the dead of night, to substantiate the wife's suspicions.

How widespread are such abuses? As the surveillance technology continues to advance, it becomes harder and harder to answer such a question. It is reasonable to assume, though, that today we can easily be spied upon and our most intimate movements or conversations seen, heard, and recorded without detection.

As former U.S. Senator Edward Long has said, "The ready availability of these [electronic surveillance] devices, their low cost, and the relative simplicity of their operation have brought the practice within the reach of persons of limited means. This has increased the amount of private eavesdropping and has made even more complicated the problem of trying to determine the extent of an already complex activity.

"No one knows the extent of private snooping going on in America today. A number of studies and surveys shed some light on the problem, but the surreptitious and unethical nature of the activity makes full disclosure unlikely."

Violations of privacy, throughout history, have caused great consternation in people. Today, the techniques are far more subtle, and therefore far more frightening.

CHAPTER 12
LAW OF THE LAND

More than any other person Thomas Jefferson, the Sage of Monticello and one of the most brilliant Americans to have ever lived, is responsible for what protection there is today against the invasion of privacy.

When Jefferson was sent a draft of the U.S. Constitution for his review and comment while he was in France as an emissary, he quickly noted that the document did not spell out an individual's rights. It was he who proposed the addition of ten Amendments to the Constitution—the Bill of Rights—to correct this omission. They were approved in 1791.

It is the Fourth Amendment that most directly pertains to privacy. It states: "The right of the people to be secure in their persons, houses, papers and effects, against unreasonable searches and seizures, shall not be violated, and no warrants shall issue, but upon probable cause, supported by oath or affirmation, and particularly describing the place to be searched, and the persons or things to be seized."

Commenting on this, Justice Louis Brandeis of the U.S. Supreme Court, said in 1928: "The makers of our Constitution . . . sought to protect Americans in their beliefs, their thoughts, their emotions, and their sensa-

tions. They conferred, as against the Government, the right to be let alone—the most comprehensive of rights and the right most valued by civilized men. To protect that right, every unjustifiable intrusion by the Government upon the privacy of the individual, whatever the means employed, must be deemed a violation of the Fourth Amendment."

It is fair to say that Jefferson, James Madison (the "Father of the Constitution"), and their colleagues believed that they had protected the people once and for all from unwarranted intrusions. But, as Senator Charles Mathias of Maryland has said, "They could not foresee the electronic age. They could not foresee telephones, wiretaps, bugging devices. They could not foresee that technology would make our homes and our private lives accessible, even when our doors are locked and our shades are drawn.

"In our century, increasingly sophisticated electronic technology spawned opportunities for unauthorized intrusions never dreamed of by the framers of the Constitution." The senator went on to say that electronic prying threatens to "burst the restraints of the Fourth Amendment."

The laws regarding electronic surveillance date back to the First World War, when the federal government took over control of the nation's telephone and telegraph systems. In an effort to provide protections both for the government and for the property of the telephone and telegraph companies, Congress, in 1918, passed a law prohibiting wiretapping or other interference with the systems. After the war, however, when private companies resumed operation of the systems, the law expired.

Above: *Thomas Jefferson.*
Below: *Louis Brandeis*

In the early 1920s, the Department of Justice used wiretapping to gain information about illegal aliens in the United States. This was allegedly halted in 1924, when Attorney General Harlan Fiske Stone banned tapping by his department. But this was the era of Prohibition, when alcoholic drinks were illegal. Not covered by Stone's decree, the Treasury Department used telephone wiretapping in its efforts to enforce the Prohibition laws. It was this practice that ultimately led to one of the country's landmark court cases involving electronic surveillance—*Olmstead* v. *the United States* in 1928.

In this instance, the defendant (Olmstead) had been convicted for conspiring to violate the Volstead Act, which was one of the Prohibition laws. Much of the evidence centered on information that had been gained by extensive wiretapping of Olmstead's telephones. Federal agents had monitored them for months.

In the lower court trial and in their presentation to the U.S. Supreme Court during the appeal process, defense attorneys contended that the tapping was contrary to the Fourth Amendment, especially the "search and seizure" clause. They also said that the wiretap evidence should not be allowed because of the self-incrimination clause of the Fifth Amendment. This states: "Nor shall [a person] be compelled in any criminal case to be a witness against himself."

This landmark case was to set a precedent in the laws and the interpretation of them regarding electronic surveillance for years to come. The Supreme Court, by a narrow five to four margin, ruled in favor of the government, allowing the Olmstead conviction to stand.

In the majority opinion, as expressed by Chief Justice William Howard Taft, the Court found wiretapping involved no physical intrusion or trespass into a home or office and no seizure of material things. It stated: "The evidence was secured by . . . the sense of hearing and that alone. There was no entry of the houses. . . . The language of the Amendment cannot be extended and expanded to include telephone wires reaching to the whole world from the defendant's home or office."

In other words, although the Court felt the Fourth Amendment gives protection to a letter in the mail, it does not allow for such protection of a telephone call. The Court majority opinion said that a letter was a "piece of paper," a material and tangible thing, and a telephone conversation was not. The Court further held that since the Fourth Amendment had not been violated, in its opinion, the arguments about the Fifth Amendment were not valid "because there was no evidence of compulsion to talk over the phone."

This historic ruling stirred up a lot of controversy, both within the Supreme Court itself and throughout the country. Dissenting Justice Oliver Wendell Holmes, for example, felt that "Government ought not to use evidence obtained and obtainable only by a criminal act." He believed that the federal agents had violated state law when they tapped the defendants' telephones.

"For my part," Holmes said, "I think it is less evil that some criminals should escape than that the Government should play an ignoble part."

But it was the minority opinion expressed by Justice Brandeis that many feel still stands as one of the most eloquent and compelling arguments against the intrusion of privacy by electronic surveillance means. "In the application of a Constitution," Brandeis wrote, "our contemplation cannot be only of what has been, but of what may be. The progress of science in furnishing the Government with means of espionage is not likely to stop with wiretapping. Ways may some day be developed by which the Government, without removing papers from secret drawers, can reproduce them in court, and by which it will be enabled to expose to a jury the most intimate occurrences of the home. Advances in the psychic and related science may bring means of exploring unexpressed beliefs, thoughts and emotions. . . . Can it be that the Constitution affords no protection against such invasions of individual security?"

Brandeis, with rare foresight, was envisioning the future possibility of some sort of electronic police state such as that created by George Orwell in his novel *1984*. Indeed, some experts say we are in danger today of creating such a "Big Brother-is-watching-you" society if technological advances are not kept pace with by law.

Following the *Olmstead* decision, a number of new bills covering wiretapping were introduced in Congress over the next few years, but none passed. Little changed until 1934, when Congress enacted the Federal Communications Act. Section 605 of that act covered some areas of electronic surveillance.

This section said, in part: "No person not being authorized by the sender shall intercept any communication and divulge or publish the existence, content, substance, purport, effect, or meaning of such intercepted communication to any person."

Although this act was designed to bring order into the rapidly growing field of radio and wire communications, it did not specifically cover wiretapping. Still, a number of "tap" cases were brought before the U.S. Supreme Court citing section 605.

Perhaps the most famous of these was *Nardone v. the United States*, which occurred in 1937. Here, the defendants' telephones had been tapped by federal agents. The defendants were convicted for smuggling and concealing alcohol.

In the Supreme Court hearing, the government argued that Congress had not intended Section 605 to prohibit tapping wires by law enforcement agents to procure evidence. The Court, however, ruled otherwise. It said, in the decision, "The plain words of Section 605 forbid anyone, unless authorized by the sender, to intercept a telephone message, and direct in equally clear language that 'no person' shall divulge or publish the message or its substance to 'any person.' To recite the contents of the message in testimony before a court is to divulge the message." Thus, the Court held the wiretap evidence inadmissible.

This decision, too, was criticized. Many felt the judicial branch of the federal government was, in effect, enacting legislation of its own. Law enforcement officers, in particular, were stung by the *Nardone* case, feeling that the inadmissibility of wiretap evidence greatly hampered their work. As a result, a number of new bills were introduced in Congress allowing wiretapping in special criminal investigations, but none passed. The government did not stop the practice of wiretapping, but for the most part, it stopped trying to use wiretap evidence in federal court.

It was more than three decades since the enactment of Section 605 before another major bill pertaining to electronic surveillance was passed by Congress. This occurred in 1968 with Title III of the Omnibus Crime Control and Safe Streets Act. This act was designed to breach the gap between the individual's rights of privacy and the needs of law enforcement agencies to use such means as wiretapping and bugging to build cases against major criminal offenders. It covered wire and oral communications.

Title III said that law enforcement electronic surveillance of conversations was prohibited except under a court order. And there were special stipulations to guide judges as to when to issue such an order. Among them were:

- application for the order by a high-ranking prosecutor

- probable cause to believe that a crime has occurred, that the target of the surveillance is involved, and that evidence of that crime will be obtained by the surveillance

- a statement indicating that other investigative procedures are ineffective

- an effort to minimize the interception.

Further, it is specified that a judge may order a wiretap if satisfied that there is probable cause for belief that an individual is committing, has committed, or is about to commit a particular crime—espionage, sabotage, murder, kidnapping, extortion, bribery, gambling, jury tampering, obstructing justice, theft from interstate shipments, counterfeiting, drug dealing, bankruptcy fraud, illegal union activities, conspiracy, or other violent felonies.

Seven years later, the Privacy Act of 1974 was passed; it attempted to deal with the growing ease of information-gathering made possible by computers. This law requires agencies to comply with fair information practices in their handling of personal information. It holds that records must be necessary, lawful, current, and accurate, and that they must be used only for the purpose collected except with an individual's consent or where exempted. Also, the information collected cannot be sold or rented for mailing-list use. However, there were a number of significant exemptions to this act. These included records of the Central Intelligence Agency, records maintained by law enforcement agencies, and Secret Service records, among others.

In 1978, the Foreign Intelligence Surveillance Act became law. It established legal standards and procedures for the use of electronic surveillance to collect foreign intelligence and counterintelligence within the United States. This set a precedent, as it was the first law authorizing wiretapping and other forms of electronic surveillance, such as radio intercepts, closed-circuit television, beepers, microphone eavesdropping, and other monitoring techniques.

As a check against unauthorized use of this act, the law called for the creation of the Foreign Intelligence Surveillance Court. This court was to be made up of seven federal district judges whose job it would be to review and approve surveillance monitoring of U.S. citizens, permanent resident aliens, and domestic organizations or corporations that were not openly known to be directed and controlled by foreign governments.

The Right to Privacy Act, also passed in 1978, provides bank customers with some privacy regarding their records held by banks and other financial institutions. But it also described how federal agencies could gain access to such records. Similarly, the Electronic Funds Transfer Act of 1980 says that any institution providing funds transfers or other bank services must notify its customers about third-party access to customer accounts.

The Cable Communications Policy Act of 1984 gives some protection to cable service subscribers. For example, cable companies must inform their subscribers of personal information collected and the nature of the use of such information as well as any disclosures that may be made of it. The act creates a subscriber right to privacy against government surveillance.

CHAPTER 13
WHAT PRICE PRIVACY?

Former U.S. Supreme Court justice Louis Brandeis once said that privacy is "the most comprehensive of rights, and the right most valued by civilized man." Yet today, in this computerized technological age, it is becoming increasingly difficult for a person to escape persistent observation or eavesdropping by a vast array of electronic surveillance devices and systems. If someone, government agent or otherwise, wants to, he or she can listen in on our most secret conversations, photograph us from great distances or in the dark, track our daily movements, or compile a mountain of information about us—without our ever knowing it.

The computer, too, has revolutionized our lifestyles. In a sense, it virtually follows us everywhere. Every time we fill out a form or buy something with a credit card, the information goes into an electronic file. And these files keep building. They are fed by school records, employment records, government records, medical records, tax records, consumer credit records, motor vehicle records, and the list goes on. You cannot escape it.

And all of this has invaded our privacy. With computers, information is easier and cheaper to store and retrieve and allows us to more easily label and categorize people. A generation ago, when records were tucked away on paper in manila folders, there was some assurance that such information wouldn't be spread everywhere. Now, however, our life stories are available for examination at the push of a button. The facts of our lives are reduced to binary bits that can be compacted into dossiers and displayed on terminal screens thousands of miles away. Further, we are told that the federal government has an average of eighteen files for each man, woman, and child in the United States, and that there are thousands of data banks containing information on nearly four billion identifiable persons. As the late U.S. Senator Sam Ervin of North Carolina once said, "Once data is collected, it is out of the individual's control and can be bought, sold, stolen or altered without the individual's knowledge."

Aside from computers, we are watched and heard in scores of other ways. Every time we walk into a department store, bank, supermarket, or convenience store, we are "on camera." Every time we call someone on the telephone, a third party may be listening in. If not directly seen or heard, our movements can be "felt" by any number of sensing systems that can detect everything from our physical movement to our body temperatures.

All this is very frightening. Of course, most of us do not think about it, nor would we be aware of such surveillance. But the fact is, the capability exists, and today, more often than not, even if we were aware of such surveillance, there is precious little we can do about it.

This is because the laws, in general, have not kept up with technology. And even where laws protecting our privacy do exist, they are, as we have seen, frequently and easily violated. For every single legal wiretap, there are dozens of illegal and unreported ones. For every legitimate callup of personal data from a computer bank, there are scores of illegitimate ones. For every proper use of electronic surveillance, there are many instances of misuse. And, as newer and more refined devices, systems, and techniques emerge, our privacy becomes even more endangered.

But there is another side to the issue. The individual's rights to privacy are on one side. On the other is the claim of law enforcement agencies, business, industry, and others that the proper use of electronic surveillance cuts down substantially on crime and allows for more secure, and therefore more efficient, operation of agencies and companies.

In its congressional report, "Electronic Surveillance and Civil Liberties," the Office of Technology Assessment addressed this dilemma:

Electronic surveillance is the epitome of the two-edged sword of technology for many Americans. Public opinion polls evidence considerable concern about possible excessive and abusive use of electronic surveillance by the government (and others), and show support for strong safeguards and protections to tightly control the use of such technology.

But, at the same time, the public is concerned about crime—especially violent crime—and supports the appropriate use of technology to combat and prevent crime and bring offenders to justice.

Until the past 10 years or so, the balancing of these concerns was relatively straightforward from a technological perspective. Electronic surveillance was limited primarily to audio surveillance devices such as telephone taps and concealed microphones ("bugs"). Now, however, technological developments have significantly expanded the range of electronic surveillance options.

These include miniaturized transmitters for audio surveillance, light-weight compact television cameras for video surveillance, improved night vision cameras and viewing devices, and a rapidly growing array of electronic communication—whether via wire, coaxial cable, microwave, satellite, or even fiber optics—can be monitored if one has the time, money, and technical expertise. Encryption—the only technological countermeasure thought at this time to be generally effective—is too expensive and cumbersome for widespread application, although costs are declining and ease of use is improving.

Further, the report states: "The capabilities for surveillance," which it describes as the observation and monitoring of individual or group behavior including communications,

are greatly expanded and enhanced with the use of technological devices. For example, technology makes it more efficient and less conspicuous to track movements, to hear conversations, to know the details of financial and other personal transactions, and to combine information from diverse sources into a composite file.

New surveillance tools are technically more difficult to detect, of higher reliability and sensitivity, speedier in processing time, less costly, more flexible and adaptable, and easier to conceal because of miniaturization and remote control. Current research and development will produce devices with increased surveillance capabilities, such as computer speech recognition and speaker identification, fiber optics, and expert systems.

From a law enforcement and investigative standpoint, the potential benefits offered through new electronic technologies may be substantial—e.g., the development of more accurate and complete information on suspects, the possible reduction in time and manpower required for case investigation, and the expansion of the options for preventing and deterring crime.

From a societal perspective, the possible benefits are also important—including the potential to increase one's sense of physical security in the home and on the streets, improve the capability to know when someone is in need of assistance, strengthen efforts to prevent the sale of illegal substances, and enhance the protection of citizens and government officials from terrorist actions.

But, the report also exposes the other edge of the "sword." It says,

However, while providing increased security, the use of sophisticated technologies for surveillance purposes also presents possible dangers to society. Over time, the cumulative effect of widespread surveillance for law enforcement, intelligence, or other investigatory purposes could change the climate and fabric of society in fundamental ways.

For example, how will hotlines that encourage people to anonymously report potentially damaging information and one-party consent to the monitoring of conversations affect the level of trust in our society? Will private space and anonymity be preserved when individuals increasingly must make private information widely available to banks, medical clinics, and credit agencies, in order to carry on everyday activities?

District Court Judge Jack Love of Albuquerque, New Mexico, displays a so-called "electronic handcuff" to be given to probation officers who will keep electronic tabs on the comings and goings of criminals on probation. At what point do we cross the line between the public's need for protection from crime and the loss of a citizen's individual freedom? It's not an easy question.

To this point, Senator Mathias of Maryland adds: "What about the growing number of Americans, who, in recent years, have been willing to trade some of their privacy for increased personal safety? Many have retreated behind walls, into closed communities, where visitors can be screened, common areas monitored, suspicious strangers challenged and ejected.

"It's easy to imagine the voters of an entire town deciding to wire their community for sound and video, and for monitoring by the all-seeing central computer. The two would bar entry to all who refused to wear a transmitting device. A society tortured by the fear of crime might establish 'Big Brother' by popular demand. Those who valued their privacy more highly could try to reverse the policy at the next election, or simply move away . . ."

According to the Office of Technology Assessment report,

The use of electronic surveillance devices may [also] infringe on the protections afforded in the first amendment [freedom of speech and press and the right to peaceably assemble and to petition the government for a redress of grievances], fourth amendment [unreasonable searches and seizures], and fifth amendment [protection against self-incrimination]. The use of such devices may also conflict with . . . protections in specific statutes.

Many innovations in electronic surveillance technology have outstripped constitutional and statutory protections, leaving areas in which there is currently no legal protection against, or controls on the use of, new surveillance devices.

Although use of some surveillance techniques requires a court order, many do not require any authorized approval and some are not even covered by . . . the fourth amendment prohibition on unreasonable searches and seizures. Additionally, the privacy and procedural rights of those subject to surveillance may also be violated, since their activities may be monitored even though no criminal suspicion was attached to them. Finally, given the unobtrusive nature of surveillance activities, it may be difficult to detect when one's rights have been violated.

Thus, the report sums up,

The use of electronic surveillance devices may result in more efficient law enforcement. Their use may be required in part by the use of more evasive and sophisticated devices by those suspected of engaging in criminal activities. Yet, the cumulative impact of the increased use of surveillance, with or without a court order, is an important consideration for any society that prides itself on limited government and individual freedom.

The key policy issue is to determine the appropriate balance between the civil liberty interests and the intelligence, law enforcement, or other governmental interests involved. In some circumstances. the law enforcement interests will be great enough to outweigh the civil liberty interest. In other circumstances, the reverse will be the case.

As for now, then, the conflict between these two interests remains unresolved. As the Office of Technology Assessment found:

The existing [laws] . . . do not adequately cover new and emerging electronic surveillance technologies. Indeed, the courts have asked Congress for guidance on the new technologies.

There is no immediate technological answer to protection against most electronic surveillance . . .

The basic argument over individual rights vs. government needs is not new. Former U.S. Supreme Court Justice Louis Brandeis spoke eloquently on the issue more than half a century ago. And James Madison, fourth president of the United States, said nearly two centuries ago: "If men were angels, no government would be necessary. If angels were to govern men, neither external nor internal controls on government would be necessary. In framing a government which is to be administered by men over men, the great difficulty lies in this: You must first enable the Government to control the governed; and in the next place, oblige it to control itself."

In setting electronic surveillance policy, Congress, the executive branch, and the courts must see that civil liberties protections for the individual are balanced against the need for government and other investigations. As Senator Mathias says, "These are intriguing and complex questions which our society has never before had to face."

Thomas Jefferson, with uncommon foresight, put his finger on the crux of today's problem with electronic surveillance, though he spoke long ago. He said, "Laws and institutions must go hand in hand with the progress of the human mind. . . . As new discoveries are made, new truths discovered, and manners and opinions change with the change of circumstances, institutions must advance also, and keep pace with the times."

CHAPTER 14

WHERE DO WE GO FROM HERE?

"In the past 20 years, there has been a virtual revolution in the technology relevant to electronic surveillance," says a special congressional report prepared by the Office of Technology Assessment.

"Advances in electronics, semiconductors, computers, imaging, data bases, and related technologies have greatly increased the technical options for surveillance activities. Closed-circuit television, electronic beepers and sensors, and advanced pen registers are being used to monitor many aspects of individual behavior. Additionally, new electronic technologies in use by individuals, such as cordless phones, electronic mail, and pagers, can be easily monitored for investigative, competitive, or personal reasons. . . . The law has not kept pace with these technological changes."

Among other things, the report cited:

- The contents of phone conversations transmitted in digital form or calls made on cellular or cordless phones are not clearly protected by existing laws.

- Data communications between computers and digital transmission of video and graphic images are not protected by existing laws.

- Electronic mail messages can be intercepted at several stages and present laws offer little or no protection.

- Laws pertaining to electronic physical surveillance, such as pagers and beepers, and electronic visual surveillance, such as closed-circuit TV and concealed cameras, are ambiguous or nonexistent.

- Laws regarding data base surveillance, such as monitoring of transactions on computerized record systems and data communications linkages, are unclear.

"American businesses have produced a marvelous array of possibilities for better and faster communication worldwide," says U.S. Senator Patrick Leahy of Vermont. "Now is the time for our legal institutions to also advance and keep pace with the times. There may have been a day when good locks on the door and physical control of your own papers guaranteed a certain degree of privacy. But the new information technologies have changed all that."

To this point, U.S. Congressman Robert Kastenmeier of Wisconsin, says, "These new modes of communication have outstripped the legal protection provided under statutory definitions bound by old technologies. The unfortunate result is that the same technologies that hold such promise for the future also enhance the risk that our communications will be intercepted by either private parties or the government. Virtually every day the press reports on the unauthorized interception of electronic communications ranging from electronic mail and cellular telephones to data transmissions between computers.

"At this moment," Senator Leahy says, "phones are ringing, and when they are answered, the message that comes out is a stream of sounds denoting ones and zeros. Nothing more. I am talking about the stream of information transmitted in digitized form, and my description covers everything from interbank orders to private electronic mail hookups.

"By now this technology is nothing remarkable. What is remarkable is the fact that none of these transmissions are protected from illegal wiretaps, because our primary law, passed back in 1968, failed to cover data communications, of which computer-to-computer transmissions are a good example.

"Similarly, there is no adequate federal legal protection against the unauthorized access of electronic communications system computers to obtain or alter the communications contained in those computers.

"Problems also exist with regard to the legal protection afforded to cellular radio telephones, electronic pagers, and the private transmissions of video signals such as that used in teleconferencing," says Senator Leahy.

Adds Senator Mathias: "Technological wizardry offers a variety of new communications media. . . . Some of the messages that these new media carry are highly sensitive. A translation of the digital bits that race across our country by wire, microwave, fiber optics, and other paths could reveal proprietary corporate data, or personal medical or financial information. The users of these networks—and that means more and more of us—expect and deserve legal protection against unwarranted interceptions of this data stream, whether by overzealous law enforcement officers or private snoops. The laws on the books today may not provide that protection."

What then can be done?

In its report, the Office of Technology Assessment says that Congress could bring new electronic technologies within the realm of Title III of the Omnibus Crime Control and Safe Streets Act by doing the following:

- Treat all telephone calls the same way with respect to the extent of protection against unauthorized interception, whether analog or digital, cellular or cordless, radio or wire.

- Pass laws protecting against the unauthorized interception of data communication.

- Pass laws protecting all stages of the electronic mail process.

- Subject electronic visual surveillance to a standard of protection similar to, or even higher, than that which currently exists under Title III for bugging and wiretapping.

The report also suggests that Congress could set up new "mechanisms for control and oversight of federal data base surveillance."

It is along these lines that Senators Leahy and Mathias and Congressman Kastenmeier have been working for the past two years to get such new legislation passed. Says Senator Leahy: "[We] have been working with the Justice Department and many individuals, businesses, and industry groups who are concerned with updating the law to better protect communications privacy."

The result of their efforts is the Electronic Communications Privacy Act. This new bill would amend the 1968 federal wiretap law by broadening protection from only voice transmissions to all electronic communications, including data and video carried on non-public systems. Protection of only common carrier telephone systems would also be broadened to include all electronic communications systems unless designed to be accessible by the public.

The bill further contains criminal penalties for unauthorized access to the computers of an electronic communication system, if messages contained therein are obtained or altered. If done for commercial gain or for malicious reasons, the crime could be prosecuted as a felony offense.

To obtain communications contained in the computers of an electronic communication system, such as an electronic mail service, the government would be required to obtain a warrant. An operator of an electronic communications system would be restricted from disclosing the contents of an electronic message except in specified circumstances or unless authorized by the person sending the message.

The bill also provides that law enforcement agencies must obtain a court order based on a "reasonable suspicion" standard before installing a pen register or being permitted access to records of an electronic communications system. The bill, say its backers, does not affect the carefully balanced provisions governing foreign intelligence surveillance contained in the Foreign Intelligence Surveillance Act of 1978.

The goal of the legislation is a familiar and enduring one: to protect the privacy of Americans against unwanted and unwarranted intrusion. And Senator Leahy adds, "These changes will go a long way toward providing the legal protections of privacy and security which the new communications technologies need to flourish. . . . The protection of communications privacy can go hand-in-hand with progress. Our job is to make both a reality. Now is the time to act."

As this book went to press, this new bill was still moving through the sometimes-slow congressional process. However, its backers were confident that realization of its need was widespread enough through the Senate and House of Representatives to effect its passage either by the time you read this or soon after.

SOURCES

BOOKS

Bernstein, Carl, and Bob Woodward. *All the President's Men.* New York: Simon & Schuster, 1974.

Long, Edward V. *The Intruders—The Invasion of Privacy by Government and Industry.* New York: Praeger, 1966.

Russell, A. Lewis. *Corporate and Industrial Security.* Houston, TX: Gulf Publishing Company, 1980.

Smith, Robert Ellis. *Privacy—How to Protect What's Left of It.* New York: Anchor Press/Doubleday, 1979.

Taylor, L. B., Jr. *Gifts from Space.* New York: Crowell, 1977.

——————. *Space Shuttle.* New York: Crowell, 1978.

——————. *For All Mankind.* New York: Dutton, 1974.

Westin, Alan, and Stephan Salisbury, eds. *Individual Rights in the Corporation.* New York: Pantheon Press, 1980.

Wise, David. *The American Police State.* New York: Random House, 1976.

MAGAZINES

"A Silver Lining for Weather Satellites," *Science*. December 1983.
"Better and Better U.S. Spies in the Sky," *U.S. News and World Report*. June 1, 1981.
"Can Eyes and Ears in Space Monitor an Arms Deal?" *U.S. News and World Report*. November 25, 1985.
"Cold War Condor," *Time*. March 16, 1960.
"The Espionage Boom," *Newsweek*. July 5, 1982.
"Foreign Intelligence Surveillance Act," *Nation*. October 29, 1983.
"High Tech Vigilance," *Science 85*. December 1985.
"Intrusion Detection Systems," *Security World*. November 1985.
"Intrusive Ears of the Law," *Nation*. June 16, 1984.
"Reagan on Bugging," *Nation*. June 4, 1983.
"Satellite Spy Photos," *U.S. News and World Report*. April 4, 1983.
"Spies in the Sky," *Popular Mechanics*. February 1984.
"25 Years of Weather Satellites," *Science*. July 1985.
"Weather Satellites—25 Years," *Weatherwise*. April 1984.
"What Manufacturers Have in Store," *Security World*. March 1985.

NEWSPAPERS

"Computer Tracks Cars for Cops," *AP/Newport News, VA Daily Press*. February 19, 1986.
"Latest Gadgets Making Snooping Easy—and Legal," *Media General News Service/Richmond Times Dispatch*. December 1, 1985.
"Space Camera Raises Privacy, Security Issues," *USA Today*. February 19, 1986.

SPEECHES

"Business, Technology, and Public Policy" by Senator Charles Mathias (Washington; October 10, 1984).

"The Constitution in the 21st Century" by Senator Charles Mathias (Los Angeles; September 22, 1983).

"Privacy 1984" by Senator Patrick Leahy (Washington; August 7, 1984).

SPECIAL MATERIALS

Constitution of the United States.

Electronic Communications Privacy Act. *Congressional Record.* Vol. 131, Num. 118 (September 19, 1985).

"Electronic Surveillance and Civil Liberties." Obtained from the Office of Technology Assessment, Congress of the United States, Washington, D.C. 20510 (1985).

"Federal Government Information Technology: Management, Security, and Congressional Oversight." Obtained from the Office of Technology Assessment Report Brief, Congress of the United States, Washington, D.C. 20510 (February 1986).

INDEX

Alarm systems, 33–36
Automatic Picture Transmission (APT), 64

Big Bird, 78–79
Blackbird, 81, 82
Brandeis, Louis, 101, 102, 103, 105–106, 110, 118
Bugs, 23, 24, 25, 46–47, 88, 90

Cameras, 27–32, 48, 49, 50, 52, 61, 64, 72, 74, 78, 81, 120
Carrier current transmitters, 25
China, 79, 83
CIA, 9, 26, 45, 46, 87, 91, 108
Civil War, 74, 86–87
Computer "chips," 51
Computer "eyes," 52
Constitution (U.S.), 101, 103–106
Crime, 28, 41, 48–50, 107–108, 112, 115–117, 123
Cuban missile crisis, 74, 75

Drug Enforcement Administration (DEA), 93

Earthquakes, 60–61, 83
Eisenhower administration, 72
Electronic Communications Privacy Act, 122
Electronic Funds Transfer Act, 109

Electronic mail, 37–39, 120, 122, 123
Ellsberg, Daniel, 92
Eye vessel patterns, 30, 31, 32

Facsimile systems, 38
"False color" techniques, 56
FBI, 41, 45, 47, 52, 87–88, 90
Federal Communications Act, 106
Foreign Intelligence Act, 108–109, 123

Geostationary Operational Environmental Satellite (GOES), 67, 68, 69
Government (U.S.), 41, 44–47, 87–94, 101, 103–109, 111, 118–123

Holmes, Oliver Wendell, 105
Hoover, J. Edgar, 88, 89, 90
Huston Plan, 92

Improved Tiros Operations Satellites (ITOS), 64, 66
Industrial espionage, 95–96, 97, 99–100
Infrared beam, 26, 28, 30, 35, 64, 72
Intrusion detection systems, 48
IRS, 44, 92

Japan, 50, 70

Jefferson, Thomas, 101, 102, 103, 118
Johnson, Lyndon, 90

Kastenmeier, Robert, 120, 122
Kennedy, John F., 74, 93
KH-11 satellite, 79
Khrushchev, Nikita, 74
King, Martin Luther, Jr., 88-90
Kissinger, Henry, 94

Landsat, 53-54, 55, 57-61
Lasers, 25
Laws, 119-123
Leahy, Patrick, 120-121, 122, 123
Long Range Navigation system (LORAN-C), 22

Madison, James, 103, 118
Mathias, Charles, 103, 116, 121, 122
McClellan, George, 74
McCord, James, 9, 10, 11
McGrath, Howard, 88
Microphones, 24, 25, 34, 88
Microwave systems, 34, 35
Military surveillance, 50, 71-85
Miniaturization, 15, 26, 27
Missiles, 72, 74, 75, 76, 77, 80, 81, 84, 86

Nardone v. U.S., 106-107
National Oceanic and Atmospheric Administration (NOAA), 67, 69
Navstar, 79-80
Nixon, Richard, 10, 12, 13, 92, 93, 94
NORAD, 77
Nuclear detection, 79, 83

Oceanography, 59, 69
Olmstead v. U.S., 104

Pagers, electronic, 20, 22, 120, 122
Passive electronic devices, 25
Pentagon Papers, 92
Perimeter-infusion detection, 50
Photoelectric beams, 34, 50
Photography, space, 55, 56, 57, 58, 61-62
Powers, Francis Gary, 71-72, 73

Privacy, 98-101, 103, 107-118
Privacy Act of 1974, 108
Prohibition, 104

Radar, 83, 84
Radio, 19, 26
Recordkeeping, computerized, 20, 21, 39, 41-43, 52, 108, 110-111
Right to Privacy Act, 109
Roosevelt, Franklin, 87

Satellite Early Warning System (SEWS), 80
Satellites, artificial, 53-62, 64, 65, 66-70, 76-81, 83
See also specific satellites
Schenley Industries, 95
Security surveillance systems, 28-30, 31, 32, 47-48
See also Alarm systems
Seismometers, 83
Shite Cloud, 81, 83
Soviet Union, 23, 71-72, 74, 76, 78, 79, 80, 83, 86
Spot 1, 61-62
Stone, Harlan Fiske, 94, 104
Supreme Court (U.S.), 104-107
Synchronous Meterological Satellite, 66, 67

Taft, William Howard, 104
Tape recordings, 10, 12, 93
Telegraph, 38, 86-87, 103
Telephones, 17, *18*, 19-20, 21, 103, 119, 121, 122
Teletext, 38
Television, 28, 29, 35, 47, 48, 49, 120
Telex, 38, 40
Thermal detectors, 34
Tiros, 64, 65

Ultrasonics, 35
U-2 incident, 71-72, 73

Vietnam War, 78, 90, 91, 94
Voice mail, 38

Watergate, 9-12, 23, 86, 87
Weather, 63-70
Wiretapping, 16, 45, 46-47, 86-87, 90-94, 103-108, 121, 122
Wise, David, 87, 93, 94

—128

DISCARDED

JUN 26 2025

TK 7882 .E2 T39 1987

89-1368

Taylor, L. B.

Electronic surveillance

ASHEVILLE-BUNCOMBE
TECHNICAL COMMUNITY COLLEGE
LEARNING RESOURCES CENTER
340 VICTORIA ROAD
ASHEVILLE, NC 28801